New Perspectives on Asian History
Series Editors Ainslie Embree and Edward Farmer

Merchants and Faith: Muslim Commerce and Culture in the
Indian Ocean
Patricia Risso

Learning to Be Modern: Japanese Political Discourse on Education
Byron K. Marshall

Merchants and Faith

*Muslim Commerce
and Culture
in the Indian Ocean*

Patricia Risso

*To Mary, who, in a way,
made me fondly, Pat
do this!*

Westview Press
Boulder • San Francisco • Oxford

New Perspectives on Asian History

Copyright © 1995 by Westview Press, Inc.

Published in 1995 in the United States of America by Westview Press, Inc., 5500 Central Avenue, Boulder, Colorado 80301-2877, and in the United Kingdom by Westview Press, 12 Hid's Copse Road, Cumnor Hill, Oxford OX2 9JJ

Library of Congress Cataloging-in-Publication Data
Risso, Patricia.
   Merchants and faith : Muslim commerce and culture in the Indian
Ocean / Patricia Risso.
      p.   cm.—(New perspectives on Asian history)
   Includes bibliographical references and index.
   ISBN 0-8133-1682-0.—ISBN 0-8133-8911-9 (pbk.)
      1. Indian Ocean Region—History.   2. Indian Ocean Region—
Commerce—History.   3. Muslims—Indian Ocean Region—History.
I. Series.
DS340.R57   1995
382'.09172'4—dc20   94-42937
                                                                                              CIP

Printed and bound in the United States of America

   The paper used in this publication meets the requirements
of the American National Standard for Permanence of Paper
for Printed Library Materials Z39.48-1984.

10   9   8   7   6   5   4   3   2

Contents

Maps

Acknowledgments and Transcription Note

Some of the research for this book was made possible by a National Endowment for the Humanities Travel to Collections grant, summer of 1992, and two Research Allocations Committee grants, summers of 1990 and 1992, from the University of New Mexico. Many people helped along the way. I am grateful to Melissa Bokovoy, Jonathan Porter, Omeed Memar, Ralph Austen, Derryl MacLean, and especially Richard Payne and William Risso. I also want to thank the series editors, Edward Farmer and Ainslie Embree; Westview Press Senior Editor Peter Kracht; Lynn Arts and Connie Oehring in Westview Press's Editorial Production Department; copy editor Beverly LeSuer; and Eric Leinberger for his excellent work on the maps.

To keep the text as uncluttered as possible, the Arabic script consonants *ayn* and *hamza* have been indicated (as apostrophes) only medially, except in quotations and titles. Subscript dots and long vowel marks have been omitted. Pinyin transcription has been used for Chinese words except for names and places better known by other spellings, such as Canton.

In cases where there could be confusion, alternate spellings are given at the first reference, for example, Quilon (Kawlam).

Patricia Risso

1 Introduction

The main focus of this book is the intersection of Islamic and Indian Ocean histories; the main purpose is to illustrate relationships among ideology, culture, and economics. The intersection is potentially a rich area for research but is complicated by subspecialty boundaries, the huge expanses of time and space, and linguistic challenges. Despite these difficulties, there is a growing body of relevant scholarly literature. Such research has generated questions that help to shape this book: What were the relationships between littoral Asia and land-based empires? How can we best explain the role played by West Europeans in the Indian Ocean region, particularly in relation to Muslims? What difference did it make to be a *Muslim* merchant?

Within the historical framework of land-based states, particularly of Islamic states, this book explores the less accessible story of maritime Asians, particularly Muslims. General histories of the Islamic world seldom draw upon research dealing with the Indian Ocean, probably because the latter is often couched in the technical language of economic theories and systems. In order to make that material more accessible to non-specialist readers and to students, this study attempts to distill some of its more significant results and connect them to well-established features of Islamic and Asian history. The emphasis on Muslims dictates the starting point of the seventh century. The mid-nineteenth century is a reasonable place to stop not just because of the consolidation of the British Empire but also because, by then, the impact of European technology was evident. Also in that century, Muslims lost their high profile in the Indian Ocean. There is no attempt to impose analytic unity on the fourteen hundred or so years covered here; rather, Chapters 2 through 5 have their own chronology and illustrate themes reflected in their titles. Chapter 2 deals with the rise, development, and especially the expansion of Islam and the dispersion of Muslims as far as the coast of China. The third chapter follows further expansion and permanent Islamization in South Asia, Southeast Asia, and East Africa during a middle era, when military states dominated the Asian landmass. Chapters 4 and 5 form a complementary pair, examining the early modern era first with an emphasis on Asian strengths and then in terms of European impact. The chapter themes are drawn together by historiographical con-

1

siderations, geography, and especially the focus on Islam. Chapter 6 offers an overview and conclusions.

Historiography

The reader will immediately notice considerable attention to historiography: sources, methods, biases, schools of thought, and especially the interpretations of individual historians that are representative of the lively debates relevant to the role of Muslims in maritime history. The purpose in frequently juxtaposing two or more scholarly views on a topic is not so much to judge between them as to draw from them whatever information or insights might help answer the questions posed here at the outset and also, simply, to illustrate the range of debate. The emphasis on historiography is appropriate because a controversial topic lends itself to—and perhaps requires—a degree of self-consciousness about the writing of history.

There is a tension that underlies the historiography of Asian and Islamic history, a tension most often generated by honest differences of scholarly opinion. An important example has to do with the premise on which historians base their questions about the past. One view is that outcomes, such as British dominance in India in the nineteenth century, suggest questions that should be asked of the preceding centuries. Such questions might be: How can the Mughal decline be best explained? What institutions or policies gave Europe an advantage over Asia? An opposing view is that the historian should not work backward, that the historian's knowledge of outcomes should not determine his or her analysis of the past. British dominance in India was not the only possible outcome and therefore should not be explained as such. What if, for example, India had not been subjected to British rule? One answer is that it would have emerged successfully, on its own terms, from the decline of the Mughal regime; such a decline was only part of a natural cycle.[1] Both approaches pose problems. In the first case, allowing outcomes to determine questions might well narrow the historian's view and, in this example, result in Eurocentrism through which British success would be ratified by the past.[2] In the second case, the historian might be sidetracked by "what if" speculations that are inherently interesting but do not contribute to an understanding of actual outcomes. However, these different approaches have the potential to maintain a healthy balance in interpretation.

Increased contact among scholars with personal backgrounds in the West and those with backgrounds in Asia has lessened a tendency toward national or culture-bound history, that is, history that elevates the role of the historian's own nation or culture. However, a small portion of the literature on Islamic history and on Indian Ocean history is marred by ideological bias, ranging from unreformed Marxism to capitalist apologetics, from assumptions of Asian moral superiority to strident Eurocentrism. No study, including this one, can be totally free of bias. Some of it is rooted in centuries-old competition, hostility, and misunderstanding between the Islamic world and Western Christendom. Some is rooted in a reaction against nineteenth-century Western hegemony in much of Asia. Perhaps the most insidious bias is that which insists on a strict dichotomy between Europe and Asia or between Christendom and the Islamic world. While such distinctions constitute meaningful shorthand, they can obscure similarities among human attitudes, behaviors, and institutions. It becomes too easy, for example, to lose perspective on what is foreign. There is often a tacit assumption that people of Asia, however different from one another they may have been in terms of culture and worldview, were all somehow self-conciously Asian and, therefore, fundamentally if vaguely the same, while Europeans represented a very alien but also internally unified group. But how much *less* foreign was an Arab peddler in ninth-century Canton than a Portuguese peddler in sixteenth-century Surat?

Geography

Geographic terminology needs to be clarified for the broad scope of this book, which encompasses East, Southeast, South, and West Asia. "South Asia" and "India" are used interchangeably to refer to the subcontinent, including modern Pakistan, Bangladesh, and the Republic of India as well as the island of Sri Lanka. "West Asia" is used as an alternate designation for the Middle East, of which Egypt is culturally and economically a part, even though it is on the African continent. "Geographic Syria" is used as a shorthand designation for what is now Lebanon, Syria, Jordan, Israel, Palestine and the remaining Occupied Territories. "Central (or Inner) Asia" is included as the homeland of the Turks and Mongols and as the avenue of caravan trade. The emphasized maritime scope is defined as the Indian Ocean region, that is, not only the littorals of the ocean itself but also the connected bodies of water, specifically the Red Sea, Persian Gulf, and South China Sea. It should be noted that a large portion of the Indian Ocean off the west coast of India is often referred to as the Arabian Sea, while a corresponding eastern portion is often called the Bay of Bengal.

The huge Indian Ocean constitutes a maritime space less cohesive than the Mediterranean; yet, the monsoons provide a degree of geographic unity.[3] In winter months, approximately November through March, high pressure zones over the Asian landmass and low pressures over the ocean produce prevailing winds blowing in a southwesterly direction from India and from China. In the summer months, approximately April to September, the pressure zones and wind directions reverse. The optimal sailing periods during the monsoons were relatively short and storms were often a problem, so mariners learned to catch the winds at certain times, depending on their points of embarkation and destination. Some historians argue that the monsoons *determined* certain historical patterns, and there is a general consensus that the monsoons made cross-cultural experiences highly likely, such as those between Arabia and East Africa and between China and island Southeast Asia. The monsoons also heightened opportunities for sailing long distances more quickly than would otherwise have been possible and thereby made the huge region seem a bit smaller. Paradoxically, the monsoons also restricted interregional contacts, since a round-trip of any distance required the better part of a year, much of it spent waiting for the wind to change direction. The time might have been even greater than that if ocean currents were a negative factor.[4]

Maritime history is, of course, largely shaped by the monsoons, by the locations of natural harbors, islands, and reefs, and by accessibility to hinterland production. Maritime history draws upon economic, political, cultural, and social data and interpretations. The maritime world can be considered on its own but cannot be totally separated from rivers and overland caravan routes that both competed with and supplied sea-lanes. Several urban centers provided points of tangency between land and sea: for example, Basra in southern Iraq and Palembang on the island of Sumatra were important inland centers connected by rivers to the Persian Gulf and the South China Sea, respectively (see Maps 2.1 and 2.3). The maritime world also cannot be separated from land-based political units. Naval campaigns, imports and exports, and investment in maritime trade all constitute links between land and sea and often between political elites and merchants.

Maritime history derives much of its substance from commerce. Indian Ocean trade, itself determined to a significant degree by geography, generated shifting human patterns, which have usually been represented on maps as the long, curving lines of sea routes connecting emporia. A more recent, complementary representation consists of overlapping circles or loops encompassing trade regions within which local monsoon activity played a unifying role.[5] Trade patterns are the avenues of cross-cultural contact, migration, conflict, and technological change and, therefore, play a part in this book.

Islam

Historians have long debated whether predominantly Muslim regions share a civilization that can meaningfully be called "Islamic" and whether "Islamic civilization" is used as too facile an explanation for historical patterns.[6] While the debate continues, it can be said that many Muslim observers, throughout history, have argued that true Islam encompasses all aspects of life, including politics and economy.[7] From that idealistic perspective, Islam provides a comprehensive view of life that easily encompasses all the various components of maritime history. This worldliness may seem strange to someone unfamiliar with Islam. Christianity's self-concept is that of a faith permeating every aspect of life, but a faith in which a distinction is maintained between the spiritual and the temporal. Maintaining this distinction requires not only ethical worldly behavior, as does Islam, but also a degree of detachment, which Islam—except perhaps in its mystical manifestations—arguably does not. Another way to approach this difference is to say that while Christianity's foremost field of knowledge is theology, for orthodox Islam, it is law, regulating everything from ritual to contracts. This type of difference extends to politics. Christians are supposed to "render unto Caesar what is Caesar's and unto God what is God's."[8] Christianity's first centuries were partly shaped by state opposition. Despite the development much later of a monarchical papacy and national churches, Christianity did not define itself as state.[9] For Muslims, the formation of a successful state under the Prophet Muhammad was part of the normative past. The power and authority undergirding the administration of divine law ideally required an Islamic state.[10] While both Christians and Muslims have had difficulty living up to their respective ideals, those ideals shaped their worldviews.

Religion provided both a significant motivation and a sense of identity for Europeans in Asia. However, a discussion of Christians, per se, in the Indian Ocean region would likely focus on the small communities started by professional European missionaries and would not have much to do with trade. In fact, the interests of missionaries were not only distinct from but sometimes in conflict with those of the European trading companies. The governing body of the British company tried hard to exclude missionaries from India because they represented an unwelcome responsibility and an intercultural loose cannon.[11] In the Muslim context, merchants were often missionaries themselves or were accompanied by them. It was usually successful merchant families who established coastal governments in South and Southeast Asia and in East Africa, and those governments were at least nominally Islamic, measuring customary practices against Islamic norms. *Initial* expansion did not bring Islamic high culture but planted the seeds for extensive Islamization. The process linked together Muslim identity and trade.

An enormous amount of scholarship rests on the premise, accepted here, that the expansion of Islam influenced maritime as well as land-based history.[12] Islam is an ethical faith providing the foundation for social and economic interaction. Furthermore, it is portable, i.e., not identified with a certain locale where animistic spirits dwell or with temples belonging to particular dieties. For these reasons, Islam is often described as especially well suited to merchants who needed to conduct complex transactions and to travel. Islam not only sustained minority Muslim merchant communities in non-Muslim regions but also attracted many merchant converts. It can be argued that Islam made possible a commercial hegemony in the Indian Ocean region. Muslim networks became so successful that they pushed aside older patterns of trade. Those merchants who were shut out or marginalized by the networks were more likely to convert: success bred success. These interpretations will receive more attention in the chapters that follow.

Another premise is that Islam, both as a belief system and as a cultural agency, provides a valid organizational focus. By no means is Islam the only possible focus. Some studies of the Indian Ocean region have been built around, for example, migration and commodity exchange along trade routes; this approach is particularly useful for areas and times that are not well documented, such as East Africa before 1500, the history of which depends heavily on archeological evidence of settlement and trade.[13] Other possible organizational emphases are economic systems, port cities, and European trading companies.[14] There have also been attempts to make the Indian Ocean itself the focus, as Fernand Braudel did for the sixteenth-century Mediterranean.[15]

The successful expansion of the Muslim community in the Indian Ocean region affected Muslim self-perceptions and greatly increased the cultural variety of Islamic expression. Islam is not a static point of reference, a constant surrounded by variables. While some basic doctrines and laws of Islam provide anchors for the tradition, their interpretation and relative importance have changed over time. Nor is Islam monolithic. Divergence of opinion about leadership and authority generated two major branches, Sunni and Shi'i Islam, and further disputes resulted in sects and subsects, many of which can be found in the Indian Ocean region. The underlying differences can be described as political, socioeconomic, and doctrinal. Yet, the branches and sects of Islam did forge a bond based on monotheism, the ideals of social and economic justice, and quite similar bodies of law. This bond was reinforced by the success of the ever-growing Muslim community. While Muslims varied in ethnicity and religious expression, they had a common Islamic identity in relation to the non-Muslims around them.

Islam's significance in Indian Ocean history is accepted here both as a premise and as an organizational focus of this book. Such acceptance does *not* mean that Islam is viewed here as a constant ideological constraint on Muslim individuals and governments. Islam helped to shape events rather than determine them. By itself, Islam fails to provide the ultimate explanation for Asian Muslim maritime successes and failures. Islam cannot be reduced to commerce, and commerce in the Indian Ocean region cannot be reduced to Muslims, but an understanding of the complex intersection of Islamic and maritime histories provides a more accurate view of both.

2 Muslim Expansion in Asia, Seventh Through Twelfth Centuries

The Rise, Development, and Expansion of Islam

The early Islamic centuries, especially from the eighth into the eleventh, have often been described as a golden age; expansion and trade figure prominently in the positive image. During this time, Muslims had a crucial impact not only over a vast land area but also in the Mediterranean basin and along the Indian Ocean littorals. Factors external to the Islamic world created opportunities that help to explain this maritime phenomenon. An example is the economic expansion of the Chinese during the Song era, discussed later in this chapter, which had ripple effects in the Middle East. But there were also factors internal to the Islamic world that contributed to Muslim maritime success. To identify these, it is necessary to look at the rise, development, and expansion of Islam.

Many historians believe that if they can identify and explain the factors behind its emergence, they will have a handle on the *nature* of Islam. One well-known Western interpretation—outside of a faith perspective but not inconsistent with one—is that early Islam provided a social rationale for a transition from a nomadic to a sedentary lifestyle in the Hijaz province of seventh-century tribal Arabia. According to this interpretation, the rise of Islam had much to do with the economic vitality of Mecca, located along a caravan route, ostensibly linking the lucrative trade of the Yemen and Byzantine Syria and bypassing the adjacent Red Sea route of antiquity. One scholar who builds on this premise is William Montgomery Watt. He depends heavily on Muslim sources, which provide the most information but many of which were written long after the events they describe. Watt says that the clans of the dominant tribe in Mecca, the Quraysh, were undergoing profound changes brought about by commercial success and sedentarization. While the previous harsh nomadic existence of their recent forebears required interdependence and collective tribal identity, the commercial situation in Mecca rewarded individual talent and initiative. The transition resulted in an uneven distribution of wealth and power, which in turn weakened old virtues and ideals and created a need for new rules. Muhammad, from one of the less successful clans of the Quraysh, met this need by preaching a message he believed he had received from God, calling for social justice and for an identity based not on clan or tribe but on a new community bound together by faith. The rules and values of this faith were preserved in what became Muslim scripture, the *Qur'an* (recitation). Thus, Watt identifies social dislocation and spiritual crisis as crucial to the rise of Islam.[1]

A challenge to Watt and to those many scholars who followed his lead comes from another Westerner, Patricia Crone, who includes in her research extra-Islamic sources which are spatially and culturally more distant from the subject than Muslim sources but which are contemporary to the rise of Islam. She finds that the trade of Mecca was unremarkable and could not have generated the wealth—or the uneven distribution of wealth—necessary to Watt's account. Crone argues that seventh-century Arabian trade was not a continuation of the lucrative, exotic trade of antiquity. Trade in western and northwestern Arabia was local and consisted mainly of mundane items such as woolen cloth and leather goods produced from the sheep and goats of the pastoral society. Furthermore, tribal values were much intact, as evidenced by the tribal context of Muhammad's own traditional biography: for example, Muhammad was protected from his enemies by his clan, the Hashimis, who were subject to a code of loyalty and honor.[2] In fact, it was Muhammad himself who challenged tribal and clan identity with his broader, more encompassing idea of loyalty to the community of believers. While Crone rejects the traditional view, she offers only a tentative replacement: perhaps Arabians were reacting in nativist fashion to territorial encroachments by the two mutually hostile imperial powers in the Middle East at the time of the rise of Islam, the Byzantines and the Iranian Sasanids.[3] These powers were sufficiently interested in Arabia to stake claims there, along the eastern and southern coasts, including the Yemen. Maritime trade must have been the attraction. For the Persians, the silver mines of Arabia also were significant, since the Sasanid silver dirham was a major currency in the region. Crone suggests that the Arabians set aside their tribal differences and united against this incursion, with Islam as a unifying ideology. They established an expansionist state by uniting tribal groups for conquest. While trade may have been on the minds of the Sasanids and Byzantines, the Arabians were concerned with the establishment of a state through conquest. For Crone, state formation is the most consistent explanation for the rise of Islam.[4]

These analyses of the rise of Islam do little to prefigure later maritime history other than to incorporate trade in one way or another. It is more fruitful to take into account the astonishing *expansion* of well-organized Muslim tribal armies far beyond the Arabian peninsula (Map 2.1). From the Byzantine Empire they conquered Egypt and geographic Syria. The defensible Byzantine border was pushed north into Asia Minor. The new Arab regime ventured out in naval campaigns to seize critical Mediterranean islands, including Cyprus and Sicily; Arab forces approached the imperial capital, Constantinople, by land and sea, but failed to take it. To the east, in Mesopotamia and Persia, the Sasanid resistance collapsed altogether in the 640s and the last Sasanid emperor was killed in retreat in 651 by some of his own men. While the pious view of the rapid expansion concludes that it was the will of God, historians seek military, political, social, and economic explanations. The last, while difficult to isolate from the previous three, is perhaps most relevant to the present study. The economic, and specifically the commercial, component has been important in most analyses of the expansion of Arabian Islam.[5] It has been argued, for example, that Islam provided the organization necessary for Arabian society to take advantage of commercial as well as political opportunities created after the regional imperial powers were in retreat.[6] Also, expansion outside the peninsula may have been significantly motivated by a desire to gain control over trade routes in Egypt, geographic Syria, Mesopotamia (Iraq), and Persia (Iran).[7] To accommodate Crone, one might modify this explanation to say that Arabians, motivated by expansive state formation, quickly *learned* how to benefit from and develop existing trade patterns.[8]

The size and complexity of the new Islamic state caused major problems. One was that Arabians were not able to rely indefinitely on their own tribal political traditions, as they had after the death of Muhammad in 632. It was necessary to borrow from existing Byzantine and Sasanid bureaucratic structure such mechanisms as tax collection, although, theoretically at least, Islamic law governed what the taxes would be. A related change affected leadership: the first few successors (caliphs) to Muhammad were supra-tribal shaykhs, selected by and from among a traditional council of elders. The office was filled from Muhammad's tribe, the Quraysh. The pressures of expansion led to the pragmatic transformation of the tribal shaykh into an imperial ruler. This change became obvious after 661 with the establishment of the first *dynasty* in Islam, that of the Umayyads (661 to 750). The traditional account is that the Umayya clan of the Quraysh tribe, the most powerful merchant group in Mecca before Islam, had been the last to accept Muhammad as a prophet and state builder. By 661, as Muslims, the clan members were

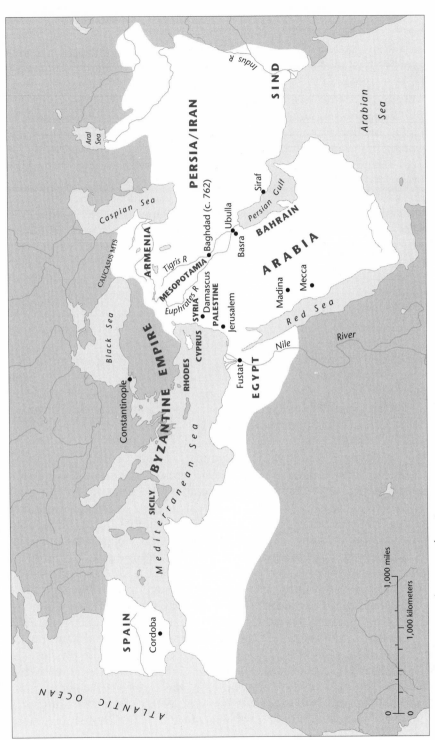

MAP 2.1 Islamic expansion, 622–circa 650

reasserting their accustomed place at the top, this time as rulers of a large expansionist state with a capital at Damascus in Syria.[9]

The stress of these changes can be seen in the emergence of a group of Muslims called the Khawarij, who tried to maintain Islam in a traditional tribal context. They took a radical, hostile stance in relation to the majority of Muslims who were making the transition to empire. Only a moderate segment of the Khawarij, the Ibadis, survived; they found homes in parts of North Africa and in Oman in southeastern Arabia.

Another problem stemmed from the desire to keep the kingdom Arab, i.e., a preserve for the tribesmen from Arabia who enjoyed the spoils of war and who held the powerful military commands. The Arabness of early Islam is easily understood, not only because of its geographic origins but also because the Qur'an refers to itself as a revelation to Arabs in the Arabic language.[10] The proliferation of Arabic is characteristic of the late Umayyad era. At first, Arabic distinguished the conquerors, then it became the language of administration and learning and began to spread widely among the subject populations, converts and non-converts alike. In former Byzantine areas, Arabic replaced especially Greek; in Iran, Arabic script and much vocabulary were adopted for the Persian language, and from that time on educated men knew both Arabic and Persian. Early non-Arab converts were willing not only to learn Arabic but also to take Arab names and seek client relationships with Arab tribes; that is, they attempted to become Arabs as well as Muslims. But soon non-Arab converts demanded equality on the basis of their own ethnicity. They wanted access to the same privileges, legal protections, and economic advantages as Arab Muslims enjoyed. Iranians, Berbers, and others exerted pressure to universalize the new order, a process that contributed to the fall of the Umayyads and that opened the door more widely for later Asian converts.

Early Islamic history also saw a shift in urban centers. The conquering Arabian tribal armies appropriated some ancient cities, such as Damascus and Jerusalem, but their leaders also built garrison towns (Arabic: *amsar;* singular, *misr*) in which to settle the tribesmen. These towns attracted goods and services and eventually became cities that replaced some former Byzantine and Sasanid urban centers. An example is Basra in southern Iraq, a site selected in order to benefit from trade at the ancient nearby town of Ubulla and to establish a defense against possible Sasanid attack from the Shatt al-Arab, the river formed by the meeting of the Tigris and Euphrates. Basra-Ubulla competed with the old Sasanid port of Siraf on the Persian coast, which was also incorporated into the Islamic sphere. Another example of a misr is Fustat in Egypt, located near the Nile just before that river fans into a delta and accessible from both the Mediterranean and Red Sea. Fustat later generated Cairo. Strategic urbanization remained highly characteristic of the spread of Islam in later centuries.

During the eras of the early caliphs and of the Umayyad dynasty, from 632 to 750, commercial aspirations played a role in determining further avenues of conquest. Expansion was clearly regarded not only as an opportunity to spread the faith, acquire booty, and enlarge the base for land taxes; it was also seen as a way to gain control over commodities, trade routes, and customs revenues. For example, the trans-Saharan gold trade provided one of several incentives to conquer Berber North Africa. Also, the conquest of Spain (by about 730) enabled Muslims to engage more successfully in western Mediterranean commerce. Some ongoing ancient trade patterns dominated by Arabs simply continued under Islam. An example is the slave trade from East Africa. Before and after the rise of Islam, Arabians—particularly the Azd tribal group of Oman in the southeastern corner of the Arabian peninsula—participated in this maritime commerce. While most if not all the southeastern Arabians converted to Islam, and then to its Ibadi formulation, they did not attempt to impose Islam or Islamic rule in the African coastal regions where they purchased slaves brought out from the interior. There was no pressing reason to exert local control until Arab settlement in East Africa became large enough to warrant administrative costs, a situation which did not occur until the thirteenth century.[11]

From the perspective of Asian maritime history, a highly significant geographical choice for conquest was Sind, the traditional Indian province encompassing the Indus delta. Sind was important to both Indian Ocean and overland trade and was a link between them. Arab Muslim attacks from southern Iraq began in 710, resulting in the incorporation of Sind as a province in the new Islamic empire. The caliphs claimed Sind until the 860s, after which Arab rulers there became independent of the Middle East. Arab Muslim dominance was displaced by Turkic Muslim conquest in the eleventh century. Meanwhile, Arabs also established related trade communities in port towns along the west coast of India and as far south as Sri Lanka.

Although both Hindus and Buddhists were well represented in Sind, early converts to Islam tended to be the latter because the Arabs created a challenge to Buddhist-controlled urban trade; in contrast, Hindus tended to be rural agriculturalists and were thus much less affected by Muslim domination. Conversion allowed Buddhists to participate in the newly emerging Muslim trade networks connecting Central Asia, South Asia, and the Middle East.[12] True Islamization, the development of Muslim faith and institutions, took place in subsequent generations. The conversion pattern suggested for Sind has possible implications for later conversion in commercial economies throughout Asia.

The Umayyads, based in distant Damascus, were still in power when the colonization of Sind began. This eastern expansion was largely the concern of their governor in Iraq, rather than of the central administration. The most direct and pressing Umayyad maritime interests were in the Mediterranean, as far away as Muslim Spain. By both land and sea, the Umayyads and Byzantines reached an impasse, and the Byzantine frontier ceased, for the time being, to be a promising one for Islam. This situation enhanced the value of the Indian Ocean region.

The Umayyads failed to meet the demands of a large, plural empire. They were overthrown by another Arab dynasty, the Abbasids, in about 750 and managed to keep for themselves only remote Spain. Like their Umayyad predecessors, the Abbasid caliphs had Arabian roots and could claim a blood relationship to the Prophet Muhammad; but they better adapted to the realities of a plural empire. Their adaptation could be seen in their incorporation of the pre-Islamic Iranian imperial traditions and their opening of a Sasanid-inspired bureaucracy to Persian Muslims. There was still an Arab elitism in the early Abbasid era, and regionalism played a divisive role. However, the development of a unifying high culture and a growing universality in Islam strengthened the society if not the regime. An important development, stimulated by piety and perhaps facilitated by the newly learned Chinese technique for papermaking, was the growth of an elite literate class. Its members were the *ulama,* the learned men of the Muslim tradition whose collective title is derived from the root verb "to know." These men often traveled widely within the Islamic world, contributing to and spreading high Islamic culture.

It was partly due to the Mediterranean impasse with Byzantium that the Abbasids moved the Islamic capital from Syrian Damascus to Iraqi Baghdad in about 762. Basra, via Ubulla on the Shatt al-Arab, became Baghdad's port, giving access to the Persian Gulf and Indian Ocean, to South Asian and Tang Chinese trade. While control over significant maritime trade certainly contributed to Abbasid success, trade alone was not enough for a viable economy. The Abbasids had chosen Iraq also because they hoped that, using East African slave labor, they could turn the marshlands of the south into a breadbasket. The failure of this plan contributed to economic problems. The Abbasids also had to contend with political fragmentation and an inability to control their own military. They were effective imperial rulers for a relatively short time, arguably only until 900. From about 950 to 1050, members of a Persian family called the Buyids were able to marshal a more effective army than that of the Abbasids, which gave them the necessary leverage to dominate the empire from behind the throne, setting a precedent for the Saljuq Turks who came after them. The Abbasids did, however, retain the title and some of the powers of the caliphate until the Mongol conquest of Baghdad in 1258. The name Abbasid, therefore, is conventionally applied to the entire period from 750 to 1258.

A characteristic of the Abbasid era—and long after it as well—was slavery, notably military but also domestic, sexual, and agricultural.[13] In the largely arid Middle East, agricultural slavery was not common, but early exceptions include the use of slaves for drainage work in the marshlands of southern Iraq and also for cultivation of date palms in Iraq and southeastern Arabia. Some slaves were also used for pearl fishing in the Persian Gulf. The major source of such non-military slaves was Africa.[14] African slaves were sometimes used as soldiers, but most were put to domestic and agricultural labor.

Military slavery came to play a large role during the ninth century, when the Abbasids, concerned about independent-minded, impermanent Arab tribal armies, began to capture and purchase slaves to serve as a stable, elite corps. Most of these were Turks from Central Asia, who were skilled horsemen and soldiers. Soon the corps grew into a regular standing army and developed political self-interests, often to the detriment of the caliphs. The Muslim provinces that broke away from the Abbasids established slave armies of their own, drawing on Central Asians, Caucasians, and East Europeans. It is difficult to estimate the number of military slaves acquired over the centuries, but it was very high, into the tens of millions. Military slaves could rise through the ranks and attain wealth and power but few actually did so; most remained rank and file and some were virtually cannon fodder.[15]

The wide use of slaves was certainly not peculiar to Islamic history; coercion was characteristic of virtually all expansive societies which required cheap service or labor.[16] A unique feature of Islamic slavery was that religious law forbade the enslavement of free-born Muslims or free-born protected (*dhimmi*) subjects. Dhimmis were the peoples with scriptures, usually considered to be Jews and Christians, who paid a higher tax than Muslims in exchange for protection within the Islamic state. Exempting Muslims and dhimmis from enslavement meant that criminals and debtors within the society could not be made slaves, as they were in many other legal systems. There are exceptional cases of Muslims being enslaved, and much later, during the Ottoman era, the Christian subject population of the Balkans was regularly forced to hand over sons to the Ottoman military as a form of taxation. However, the ideal required that slaves be brought in from the outside through capture or purchase, making large-scale slave acquisition dependent on conquest and external—often maritime—trade.

An internal Islamic development also marked the early Abbasid era. This development was the emergence of two overlapping orthodoxies based on trends evident in earliest Islam. One was later called the Sunni tradition, which recognized authority in the Qur'an and *sunna* (custom) of Muhammad and to some extent in the consensus of the community or of its ulama. The Sunni caliph was supposed to be a political and a military leader, also responsible for the administration of Islamic law. He had no prophetic capacity, since that had ended with Muhammad. In the second half of the ninth century, the Abbasids finally came down on the side of emerging Sunni orthodoxy. The other major trend placed authority within the prophet's family, eventually limiting it to descendents of Muhammad's cousin and son-in-law, Ali. This group was called the *shi'a* of Ali, meaning the faction of Ali, from which we get Shi'i or Shi'ite Muslims. They believed that Ali and his descendents *should* have been the caliphs, in succession, by virtue of Muhammad's designation and a divinely given capacity for infallible rule. To distinguish these men from those who actually held the caliphate, they were given the title *imam*.[17] The Buyids, mentioned earlier, were of this imami persuasion, but realizing that the Sunni Islam of the Abbasids was widely held, they generally did not try to impose their own doctrines. In addition to the Qur'an and sunna, the Shi'is regarded the imams' teachings as authoritative. The majority of Shi'a believed that there were twelve imams, beginning with Ali—hence their nickname, Twelvers. They believed that the last imam, born during a period of Abbasid persecution, went into a state of occultation in the 870s. Shi'is awaited (and still await) his return, at which time he would institute perfect rule. A minority of Shi'a, called Isma'ilis, accepted a different line of succession beginning with their choice of seventh imam, Muhammad ibn Isma'il; they also believed that the imamate was (and is) continuous. A group of Isma'ilis came to political power in Egypt in the tenth century as the Fatimid dynasty, and the significant contributions of this group to maritime history are discussed later.

The Sunni and Twelver Shi'i orthodoxies theorized about authority differently, but they both codified and enshrined law as the expression of God's will. The large Sunni branch of Islam eventually settled on four major schools of law—Maliki, Hanafi, Hanbali, and Shafi'i—named after early legal scholars and distinguished by their approaches to jurisprudence.[18] In the Shi'i branch, schools of legal thought corresponded to subdivisions, or sects. The majority Twelver school was called Ja'fari, after the sixth imam, Ja'far al-Sadiq. Each legal system developed a limited sense of internal cohesiveness and sometimes functioned as a political network.[19] Both branches of Islam and their respective schools and subgroups diverged somewhat in their legal interpretations, but their bodies of law and precepts were more similar than different.

This legalistic development, well under way by the early tenth century, had two major consequences relevant to expansionist maritime history. First, the emphasis on the administration of law provided the possibility for secure and stable conditions wherever Islam spread and provided a common legal system over a large area. Second, Muslims took with them the ideal if not the studied practice of rules which governed all aspects of life, including war and commerce. Behaviors based on this ideal were usually evident enough to identify *as Muslims* peoples of various languages and ethnicities. In other words, Muslim identity was based not only on certain beliefs and rituals but also on specific social and commercial behaviors.

The emphasis on law and its application contributed to the widespread popularity of mysticism (sufism), as people sought to augment or replace dry legalism with a direct experience of God. Sufis traced their inclination back to the Prophet Muhammad, who, according to tradition, practiced solitary, meditative prayer. The first historical evidence emerged in the eighth century, when the practice was ascetic and individualistic. Later, sufis began to organize themselves into orders or brotherhoods based on the teachings of a particular master or saint, and such orders flourished especially between the eleventh and sixteenth centuries. Large membership and social rituals often diluted sufism into a popular, heterodox form of Islam. In cities, educated sufism and orthodoxy found common ground, but, in the countryside or at a distance from orthodox political control, sufism retained its heterodox ways. On the frontiers, where Islam came up against other religious traditions, the non-doctrinal, often eclectic ideas and practices of sufism were effective in attracting converts to Islam. Sufis usually remained involved with the world, stimulating political reform movements and even generating new regimes. Many brotherhoods encouraged trade by offering hospitality to merchants and other travelers along caravan routes and at ports.

Law, however, remained the backbone of orthodoxy. The Qur'an was the primary source of law, but there is very little in that scripture directly related to maritime regulation. Merchant ships are mentioned as a sign of God's bounty, and such references are clearly positive. Three examples are:

> Surely in the creation of the heavens and the earth; in the alternation of night and day; in the sailing of ships through the ocean for the profit of mankind ... here are signs for a people who understand. (Qur'an 2:164)

> It is He who has made the sea subject [to you] that you might eat fish from it and that you might extract from it ornaments to wear; and you see ships ploughing in it that you may seek [profit] from His abundance and that you may give thanks. (16:14)

Among His signs are that He sends the winds as tokens of glad tidings so you may sample His mercy; that ships may sail by His command so you may seek His bounty and be grateful. (30:46)[20]

The Qur'an also includes admonitions about fair practices in the marketplace, such as: "Fill the measure when you measure and weigh with balanced scales; that is fair, and better in the end" (17:35).[21] So explicit a directive helped give rise to an official function, that of the market inspector, the *muhtasib*, whose job it was to check weights and measures, oversee local transactions, approve medical service providers, and make sure that people in the streets observed the appointed prayers and fasts.[22]

The Qur'an forbids *riba,* "increase," translated as "interest" and usually applied broadly, although some jurists made a distinction between acceptable interest and usury. Merchants did find ways to meet the letter if not the spirit of the law by involving third parties or refiguring interest as profit. Also, Muslim moneylenders, called *sarrafs,* emerged very early in Islam.[23] Yet, the ideal of prohibiting riba was still a distinguishing feature of the Muslim community.

From the late Umayyad and the Abbasid periods, there are extant biographical materials on Muhammad. In these, his occupation was established as caravan manager, rendering trade a model livelihood. Another type of literature that developed was the *hadith,* a report of an opinion or action attributed to Muhammad. Among such reports were sayings highly favorable to merchants, such as: "The truthful, honest merchant is [on a level with or in the company of] the prophets and the truthful ones and the martyrs."[24] This sentiment was consistent with the Qur'an. It may be that a growing merchant class, overlapping somewhat with governing officials and the military, was validated by these reports.[25] Hadith literature constituted the sunna, or custom, of Muhammad and was used as a source of law, supplemental to the Qur'an.

During this same era, jurists elaborated laws that would affect maritime commerce. In addition to the strictly religious sources for jurisprudence, there were pre-Islamic and extra-Islamic customary laws that provided standards in areas such as convoy, salvage, and fishing.[26] From the ancient world, Islam had inherited types of credit arrangements, similar to bills of exchange, and also types of partnership for the purposes of trade. These were now codified in Islamic jurisprudence. A variation on simple partnership was the *commenda,* possibly of Arab origin, in which investment and liability were apportioned in a particular way.[27] Jurists also established a hierarchy of customs rates. Muslims were to charge other Muslims two and a half percent of value on goods. (This amount was one-quarter the tithe, which was a tenth part of the produce or income reserved for God, a concept already familiar in the Judeo-Christian tradition.) Muslims were to charge the protected peoples, dhimmis, five percent ad valorem. Non-protected non-Muslims, peoples subject to conquest and conversion, were to be charged the full tithe.[28] Although this system was not always employed, its exclusionary potential is clear; it also had implications for the development of Muslim networking. Both the prohibition of interest and networking will be pursued in specific contexts, especially in Chapter 4.

Reorganizations in the Tenth Through Twelfth Centuries

An important event in the tenth century was the establishment of an extensive Isma'ili trade network, accomplished mainly by a regime called the Fatimids (Map 2.2). The Isma'ilis were that minority sect of the Shi'i tradition who believed the imamate to be continuous. They also believed that the imam should actively strive to take his rightful place as leader of all Islam. Fatimid history goes back to the ninth century, when several Isma'ili communities emerged after a period of obscurity. Some grew at the geographic edges of the orthodox Islamic world in places that enjoyed lucrative maritime trade: the Yemen, the old eastern Arabian province of Bahrain, as well as Sind and Gujarat in South Asia. One group emerged in Syria, where it was difficult to win converts because most people were already committed to either the Sunni or Twelver Shi'i orthodoxies. The Syrian group, therefore, migrated to North Africa, in modern Tunisia, in the early tenth century, and proclaimed an Isma'ili imamate under a dynastic name taken from the woman who was Muhammad's daughter and Ali's wife, Fatima. This frontier region was not decidedly orthodox, so the Isma'ilis could more easily attract converts. They were also positioned to benefit from trans-Saharan and Mediterranean trade; commercial revenues were used to build military strength, including a significant navy.[29] By 969, the Fatimids were able to conquer Egypt from a minor Muslim regime. Egypt had for some time already been independent of Abbasid control from Baghdad. Under Fatimid rule, it would become a major player in the Islamic world. Perhaps because of their North African experience and because of the Isma'ili dispersion to critical ports, the Fatimids chose to expand their economy through wide-ranging trade rather than rely solely on the agricultural infrastructure of the Nile basin. They built a new capital city adjacent to the old garrison town of Fustat and called it the Victorious, *al-Qahira*, anglicized as Cairo. This city quickly became a cultural center and a base for expanded trade and proselytizing in places as diverse as Sicily, western India, the Yemen, and Bukhara in Central Asia.[30]

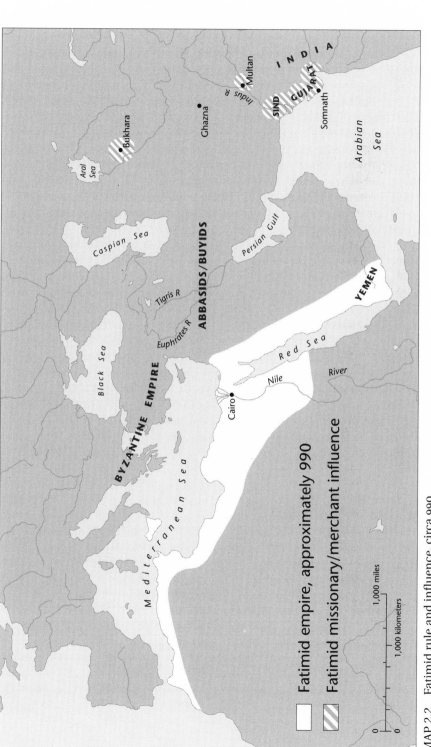

MAP 2.2   Fatimid rule and influence, circa 990

Naval capacity was essential to the Fatimids not only because of trade but because there was intense competition in the Mediterranean. Rivals included the Sunni Umayyads of Spain and resurgent Europeans who were beginning to take back islands and ports lost to Arabs in the era of Islamic conquest. The Byzantines retook Crete in 961 and Cyprus in 963. The Umayyads of Spain collapsed in 1031, after having ruled from the sophisticated capital city of Cordoba for about two hundred and seventy-five years. Subsequent Muslim political power in Spain was fragmented, allowing more economic and political opportunities for Iberian Christians. Elsewhere in the Mediterranean region, Polermo on Sicily was taken from the Fatimids by the Normans in 1072. During the last decade of the eleventh century, the Crusades began, in which Venice played an assisting maritime role.

The stiff European competition in the Mediterranean helps explain Fatimid interest in the Indian Ocean. The Fatimids took advantage of existing Isma'ili communities, particularly in Sind and Gujarat. The Fatimids benefited from the far-flung Isma'ili network, which channeled Indian Ocean trade to Cairo. Most hurt by this new competition was Abbasid Baghdad, as maritime commerce shifted from the Persian Gulf to the Red Sea, even though coral reefs made the Red Sea more difficult to navigate.[31] The patterns of trade established during this period outlived the Fatimids, who fell in 1171; for several centuries to come, Cairo would play a major role in the trade of the western Indian Ocean.

The Abbasids felt the effects of commercial competition during this era. They also experienced the political fragmentation of their empire, some examples of which have already been given. Muslim Spain had never belonged to the Baghdad caliphate; Egypt and North Africa separated themselves under various regimes, notably under the Fatimids. Much of eastern Iran and Central Asia had local Muslim rulers, such as a regime called the Samanids, who ruled throughout the tenth century from the city of Bukhara and who patronized Persian Islamic culture. Sind had independent Arab rulers by 861. An Arab Shi'i tribal confederation rendered much of Syria virtually separate in the tenth century. The Buyids exercised influence in western Iran and in Baghdad from about 950 to 1050. In the second half of the eleventh century, Saljuq Turks from Central Asia would take much of the Middle East for themselves and begin another reorganization of power.

Political fragmentation was, however, accompanied by continued commercial growth and cultural flowering. Like Fatimid Egypt, most provinces that had separated themselves from the Abbasid regime competed economically with Baghdad and with each other, a circumstance that could be inefficient but which could also stimulate trade. Each independent entity built up its own capital city, thereby enhancing the general trend in the Islamic world toward urbanization and urban consumption. The wealth of each city attracted learned and artistic men who required patronage and who could make the city a center for high Islamic culture. Geographically extreme examples are Cordoba in Umayyad Spain (until 1031) and Samanid Bukhara in Central Asia (until 999). The growth of Fatimid Cairo, a center of Arab Islamic culture, was perhaps the most important and lasting result of this far-flung urbanization.

A final change that occurred in this era was an incursion into Hindu India by Turkic Muslims from Central Asia, led by one Mahmud ibn Sebüktegin. Mahmud emerged from the slave-army that had been in the service of the Samanids. He reconsolidated Samanid territory and expanded further into Central Asia. He also led raids—reportedly seventeen—into northern India and seized booty and slaves. These raids enabled him to enlarge his military and to enrich his capital city of Ghazna in what is now Afghanistan. (He and his successors are, therefore, referred to as the Ghaznavids.) India had long been accumulating tempting wealth. Largely self-sufficient, India had been able for centuries to export cloth, timber, and grain in exchange for gold, much of which found its way to temples. Mahmud and his forces sometimes destroyed Hindu temples in the process of looting them, notably one at Somnath, on the western coast, in 1026.[32] While Mahmud governed the territories he had conquered in Iran and Central Asia, his incursions into northern India were generally hit and run, not followed by much settlement or administration. It is difficult to extrapolate Mahmud's commercial ambitions, but it is important to note that he targeted Isma'ili towns in order to gain control over their trade. The justification was that the Isma'ili sect had to be eradicated.[33] While Mahmud is not a figure in the history of maritime Asia, his regime is still worthy of attention here because his career marked the first significant Central Asian Muslim involvement in India; the Ghaznavids paved the way for Muslim rulers in much of India, especially the Sultans of Delhi and the Mughal Shahs, some of whom would play a role in Indian Ocean history.

Muslim Trade in China, Tang and Song Eras

During the centuries already covered in this chapter, Middle Eastern and Indian Muslims had contacts with China which provide remarkable evidence of the Muslim role in the maritime history of Asia. Muslims participated in the China trade not as the result of conquest but due to the demand for their services as carriers. A prominent scholar of Indian Ocean history, K. N. Chaudhuri, has identified as a "fortunate coincidence" the emergence of two new political and economic orders: the establishment of Muhammad's state in Arabia, at Madina (622), and the founding of the Tang dynasty in China (618).[34] Not since the era of the Roman and Han empires had there been this potential for political and economic stability. This coincidence is consistent with a contention, advocated here, that it is impossible to be accurate about the history of the Muslims in the Indian Ocean without giving China its due.

Before the rise of Islam, the Chinese most often dealt with maritime merchants from South Asia, who were then dominant in the Indian Ocean region and who built the best vessels available. After the rise of Islam and its expansion along the west coast of India, China's carrying trade shifted from Hindu and Buddhist *Indians* to Arab, Persian, and Indian *Muslims.* The vessels used in this trade continued to be, for the most part, South Asian but later were often built in China itself.[35]

The Tang dynasty reorganized China in centralist fashion after a period of political fragmentation. Its capital was the large, sophisticated city of Chang'an, modern Xian, in Shaanxi province. Tang rulers built anew upon the bureaucratic foundations dating back to the ancient Han dynasty. The first—and strongest—Tang century, roughly 618 to 700, was characterized by demographic change: economic and territorial pressures led to a shift of China's population from the north to central and southern regions, where there were more agricultural and coastal commercial opportunities. There continued to be active trade along the Silk Road to the west-northwest through Central Asia, but now also maritime trade was sought, especially in the south.

This new emphasis on trade was somewhat incongruous with China's theoretical view of its own socio-economic structure. In contrast to Islam's favorable attitude toward commerce, Confucianism accorded very low status to merchants, who were regarded as parasites dependent on the production of others. In the real economic world, trade was a necessity and merchants could in fact make large sums of money and wield influence. Confucian governments usually found ways to tolerate and even encourage merchants while at the same time taxing them rather heavily in order to maintain leverage.

Throughout the Tang period, there were numerous foreigners who traded to and sometimes lived permanently in China. Several ports and inland cities were officially open to foreign merchants, who could be found in less prominent locations as well.[36] China already had a cosmopolitan population that incorporated, for example, the different beliefs and values of Daoism, Confucianism, and imported Buddhism. The foreign merchants represented an even wider range of ethnicity and beliefs: Manichaean Uighur Turks from Central Asia, Mazdeans and Nestorian Christians from Persia, Hindus and Buddhists from both South and

Southeast Asia, and the Japanese and Koreans, who tended to adopt the Confucian and Buddhist models of China but who had their own traditions as well. There is considerable literary evidence of merchants from Siraf and Omani ports trading on the coast of China during the early Abbasid period.[37] Foreigners were officially restricted from mixing with the Chinese population but were often granted freedom to function within their own merchant communities. The Chinese emperor demanded the payment of tribute in exchange for the privilege to trade, but the amount was usually not onerous, and often those paying tribute received valuable gifts to encourage them to stay.[38] Foreigners were there to buy Chinese silk, ceramics, and porcelains for Asian markets and to supply China's growing demand for exotica. In the Tang era, a taste for foreign luxuries such as jade, ivory, frankincense, and even Persian silk spread from the imperial court to provincial nobles and urban elites.[39]

Between 755 and 763, an internal rebellion preoccupied the Tang; during that time, they lost to tribal peoples in the northwest a large degree of control over caravan routes. Even before this, in 751, they had suffered a surprising defeat at the hands of Muslims at Talas, deep in Central Asia.[40] Not only did this defeat further reduce Tang access to western Asia, it also opened the door to the spread of Islam into Chinese-controlled Turkestan and contributed to the development of a Muslim Chinese group called the Hui, who eventually scattered throughout China.

All the changes at China's northwest frontier shifted more and more commercial effort to southern China's ports, where there were significant numbers of Arab and Persian Muslims and other foreigners who were intent on trade. Even along the more hospitable coast, there were sometimes hostilities in the foreign enclaves. In 758, for obscure reasons, foreign Muslims in Canton (Guangzhou) came into conflict with the local authorities and sacked the port city. The devastation caused Canton to lapse into backwater status for about forty years.[41] But this disruption was certainly not on the same scale as the tribal contests in the northwest along the caravan routes.

The last century of Tang rule, approximately 820 to 907, was characterized by inflation, drought, plague, and rebellion. An emperor called Wuzong, who ruled from 840 to 846, put the blame for China's social problems on foreign ideologies; he encouraged the persecution of Buddhism especially and also Manichaeanism while favoring indigenous Daoism. Persecution solved nothing and only increased China's social problems. Among the rebellions against the Tang, the most notable was that led by one Huang Chao. He, too, blamed foreigners for China's problems, particularly their economic clout made possible by China's open policies. Taking a direct approach in his bid for power, Huang Chao sacked the rebuilt city of Canton in 879, killing many people and expel-

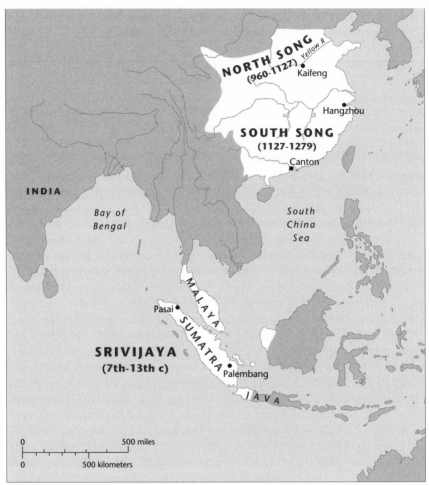

MAP 2.3   East and Southeast Asia, Song era

ling the foreigners there, including a number of Muslims. Once again, trade at Canton was seriously impaired. Expulsion and violence did not have the intended effect. Although Huang Chao went on to attack the inland capital, Chang'an, both he and the Tang regime rapidly lost power.[42] The painful events of 879 did not permanently disrupt Muslim trade in China, but things would never be quite the same.

When the Song dynasty came to power in 960 (Map 2.3), with its first capital at Kaifeng in the north, the regime enacted policies to encourage both government and private trade. Since private trade was officially regulated, it was not always easy to distinguish between the two categories. Control of the overland routes in the northwest was still problematic; the population shift to the south, evident in the Tang era, continued. Unlike the Tang, the Song set out to build a navy; they were largely motivated by the need to protect commercial vessels from piracy, which apparently had grown along with maritime trade. Shipping had improved in the Tang era, but now maritime technology advanced by leaps and bounds. There was successful experimentation with keels, rudders, and sails; navigation techniques improved; and vessel size increased, with the largest of the new ships called whales. The government ran several shipyards, and there were private ones as well. By the end of the eleventh century, Chinese vessels dominated the shipping of East Asia.[43] The Southeast Asian term *jong,* anglicized as *junk,* was later used for a range of these Chinese vessels.[44] Specific policies which enhanced this new shipping capability involved dredging harbors, improving inland waterways, fixing duties, encouraging foreign trade missions, and establishing maritime trade commissions at various ports, beginning in 971.[45]

These developments coincided with increased agricultural and industrial production, which was the result of improved technology and changes in economic policy. The most important example of the latter was a shift to a money economy, begun back in 731 by the Tang. In 749, the government had collected less than four percent of its revenues in money, but in 1065, under the Song, the proportion was over fifty percent.[46] Money was available for large-scale investment in improved production of surpluses for export. Surpluses included some agricultural items, paper, silk, and other textiles, ceramics and porcelains, and iron and steel. Northern China had been producing steel since the eighth century; by the eleventh, steel was crucial to China's economy. Steel was, of course, stronger than iron for agricultural tools and weapons and, therefore, much in demand. Large-scale steel production meant there was enough not only for domestic use but also for export, from which even China's enemies benefited.

While the Song period has been called an economic revolution or even an economic miracle, not everything went well. While revenues increased, so did expenditures to maintain the ever-growing bureaucracy and military. Despite prosperity, there was corruption in the government. Also, paper money had been officially introduced in the eleventh century, and while it offered flexibility, it often caused inflation. The most obvious problem, however, was the rise of foreign states in territory claimed by the Song: first there were the Mongolian Khitan, extending south of the Great Wall, during the tenth and eleventh centuries; then came the Tungusic Jurchen people, who, by 1127, had conquered much of northern China. The Song were forced to flee southward and establish a new capital city at Hangzhou. Having thus lost some of their industrial regions, they had to depend more on agriculture and maritime trade.[47]

How did all this affect Muslim maritime history? Both the larger amount of surplus for export and the greater reliance on maritime trade resulted in the stimulation of commerce in the South China Sea and the Indian Ocean. The ripple effects were felt in India and the Middle East. On the other hand, Chinese shipping capacity had grown and more Chinese mariners were carrying their country's products themselves. Chinese merchants began to establish permanent communities throughout Southeast Asia.[48] Still, foreign Muslims and Chinese converts to Islam were prominent as merchants and probably carried a proportional share of goods. One of the difficulties in assessing relative shares of increased trade is that most ships were built in India or China, but the owners were diverse and difficult to identify. Vessels built in the Middle East, including dhows, with flexible sewn hulls, *could* make the journey to and from China, but most Middle Eastern merchants preferred larger vessels that had watertight bulkheads and were made with iron nails. We know of one influential Arab Muslim merchant active in China early in the twelfth century who owned China-built vessels.[49] Between 1159 and 1161, and again in 1174 and 1189, there were instances of China-built vessels being force-loaned to the Song navy; the owners were of both Chinese and Middle Eastern background.[50] Fleets of China-built vessels sailed from China to India and to the Persian Gulf in the Song era. Official Abbasid ambitions for the China trade may have waned as the Middle Eastern empire fragmented and weakened after 900, but Muslims operating *from* China continued to be prominent well into the twelfth century, although their numbers are, apparently, impossible to determine.

Conclusion and Observation

The initial rise of Islam cannot be explained convincingly in terms of trade, but the directions of Islamic expansion correlate well with commercial opportunities and ambitions. During the period covered by this chapter, the bulk of Muslim maritime activity occurred in the Mediterranean and the *western* half of the Indian Ocean; maritime activity in the latter was determined largely by territorial conquest in Sind and the establishment of Middle Eastern Muslim enclaves along the west coast of India. Trade contacts with Tang and Song China expanded Muslim horizons even further.

While Muslims were important in the China trade as carriers, the eastern half of the Indian Ocean in general was still controlled by non-Muslims. The eastern coast of India was overwhelmingly Hindu. Southeast Asia was dominated by the Hindu-Buddhist kingdom of Srivijaya, whose maritime fortunes were tied to those of China.[51] Srivijaya was powerful between the sixth and thirteenth centuries. Although its trade with South Asia was undermined in the eleventh century by the fleet of the south Indian Chola regime, its China trade continued to be important into the 1200s. Some foreign Muslims who had been expelled from Canton in 879 resettled in Srivijayan territory, but the larger part of Muslim immigration to Southeast Asia came later, from India. Not until the thirteenth century would the eastern half of the Indian Ocean also be drawn decisively into the Muslim sphere.

3 Merchants of Faith in the Middle Era, Circa 1050–1500

The specifically maritime history of Muslims during the eleventh through fifteenth centuries is substantial but seems at first glance to defy the political history which is so firmly attached to land. Sketches of imperial history, given in this chapter, reveal both disinterest in maritime affairs and significant interconnections between land and sea. The Asian maritime expansion of Islamic commerce and society was brought about in a variety of ways conveyed in this chapter: foreign Muslim merchants enjoyed positions of privilege in China's ports under the early Yuan dynasty; independent merchants relocated far distances from Islamic centers of power and established networks among themselves; Muslim-dominated port towns enacted policies to cultivate and dominate regional trade.

Central Asian Expansion

Events in this era which had the most far-reaching effects in the Islamic world were the political reorganizations accomplished by Turks and Mongols from Central (or Inner) Asia. For obvious geographic reasons, these Asians did not bring with them any naval heritage. Some of the tribal groups had learned effective military organization and weapons technology from proximate imperial powers; notably, it was the Mongols who learned from the Chinese to use explosives, although it was still cavalry tactics and archery skills that won battles. The Central Asian style of rule was one in which military prowess—rather than administrative skill—took precedence and in which the benefits and privileges of power were largely confined to the military institutions. For example, one such benefit for officers in the Middle East was the wide distribution of land grants (*iqta istighlal*) with rights to land revenues, an adjustment of an old tax farming system. The grants were supposed to be temporary and revocable but tended to become de facto hereditary holdings, highlighting the land-based nature of resources and power.[1] The new Central Asian tribal elite went beyond the military-slave system introduced by the Abbasids in the ninth century, opting to rule with increasing directness rather than to settle for behind-the-scenes power.

Among the earliest military states in the Middle East were those of the migrant-conqueror Saljuq Turks who, in about 1050, replaced the Buyids as military rulers in the name of the Abbasid caliph. The Buyids had introduced the military iqta, and the Saljuqs spread its use widely. At first, the Saljuqs maintained a unified supremacy in much of the Middle East; only the Fatimids in Egypt held them off. This extensive military rule interrupted the political fragmentation process begun in the ninth century. Competition within the ruling family, however, produced separate Saljuq tribal states and principalities in Asia Minor (at the expense of the Byzantines) and in geographic Syria; only the Iran-Iraq region remained politically coherent under the major line of Saljuqs. The rulers used the title *sultan,* roughly, "holder of power." The Abbasid caliphs in Baghdad continued to represent the authority of Islam, but the Saljuq sultans took responsibility for political and military decisions. Unlike the Twelver Shi'i Buyids who preceded them or the contemporary Isma'ili Shi'is of Fatimid Egypt, the Saljuq elite joined the Abbasids in patronizing mainstream *Sunni* Islam in the context of Arabo-Persian culture.

The revenues from conquered territory and caravan routes became the assets of the Saljuqs and the other new military regimes. In return, the conquerors patronized those elements of the host culture they found useful or important, such as law and history. The type of government resulting from the Central Asian tribal infusion has been called the military patronage state because power and wealth were channeled through the army.[2] Legitimation came primarily through military success, with only a facade of religious sanction. From the point of view of the indigenous populations, the downside of political reorganization imposed from outside was the narrow range of government concerns. Increasingly left to their own devices, subject peoples turned to local institutions, such as guilds and sufi brotherhoods, to provide a sense of social organization. Also, the military regimes restricted access to power. Among the people who felt themselves shut out of political roles were the merchants, a group that had been growing and prospering since the rise of Islam.[3] In light of such an environment, it is easy to understand the independence of action that characterized many Muslim merchants during the middle era.

Land-Based Powers and Their Maritime Concerns

Mongols

The historian's imagination is perhaps most taken with the seemingly larger-than-life Mongols, who are credited with establishing quintessential military patronage states in the thirteenth century (Map 3.1). Although these steppe nomads lacked their own urban culture, they had a shamanist religion and a written legal code, the *yasa*. Exposure to Nestorian Christianity and especially to Buddhism and Islam was not uncommon, and trade contacts with Central Asian cities widened Mongol horizons. The armies of Chinggis Khan (Supreme Ruler) and his successors conquered Central Asia, China, southern Russia, some of Eastern Europe, and the Persian cultural zone in the Middle East; in each area, different branches of the ruling family dominated. Northern China had already been lost by the Song to the Jurchen in the twelfth century and then it fell to the Mongols in the 1230s; Beijing became the center of Mongol administration by 1264. The Song loyalists put up a stiff resistance from the south, based at the port capital of Hangzhou. A story of defection illustrates the undermining of Song resistance. The defector, named Pu Shougeng, was a Muslim superintendent of maritime trade at Quanzhou, a secondary Song port. He redirected the shipping under his supervision and the revenues of his port to his new master, Khubilai Khan, grandson of Chinggis Khan. These actions appear to have made a difference in the balance of power.[4] By 1279, the Mongols incorporated southern China, putting an end to the Song altogether and gaining the port of Hangzhou, which already had a large Muslim merchant community. In the midst of consolidating their vast territorial conquests, the Mongols enlarged the Song imperial navy, which had fallen into their hands. They attempted naval invasions of Japan but were thwarted by Japanese defense and *kamikaze* (divine wind) storms. A naval expedition to Java met with technical success and increased the Chinese diaspora in Southeast Asia but failed to achieve political supremacy.[5] The *naval* endeavors of the Mongols were inconclusive and the regime remained land-based.

The Mongols took for themselves a Chinese dynastic name, Yuan, and were persuaded by administrative necessity to perpetuate Chinese institutions such as civil service examinations and the tax system, but they also maintained a legal and cultural distinction between the Chinese and themselves. For example, they chose Tibetan over Chinese Buddhism and forbade intermarriage. Although they needed Confucian

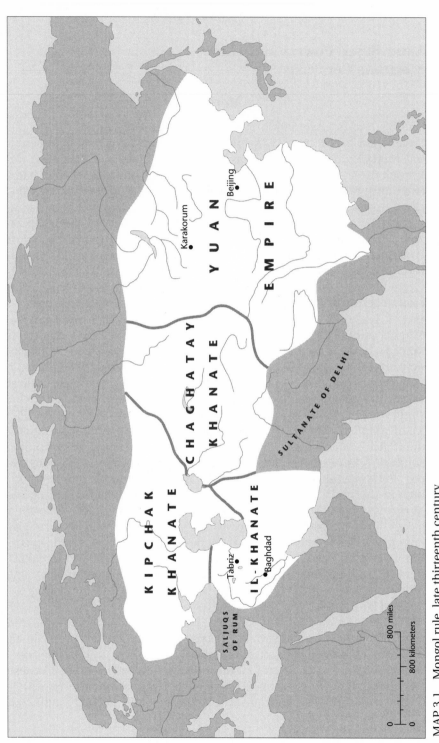

MAP 3.1   Mongol rule, late thirteenth century

Chinese bureaucrats for their expertise, the early Yuan did not wish to be overly reliant on them and so included in their administration a significant number of Muslims—some of them foreign. Muslims served as tax collectors and moneylenders. In these capacities they gained a reputation for oppression and, therefore, absorbed much hostility that might otherwise have been directed at the Yuan.[6] In southern ports, they served in disproportionate numbers as trade commissioners and superintendents of shipping.[7] The larger Muslim community in China benefited from this situation, especially in terms of trade opportunities: Marco Polo, who lived and worked for the Yuan Khubilai Khan between 1275 and 1292, reported that Muslim participation in commerce was substantial.[8] The Yuan needed the Muslims but were wary of their influence and worried about the negative reactions among the Confucian-Buddhist subject population, who resented Muslim privileged status. Therefore, Yuan policy toward Muslims vacillated, and occasionally restrictions were placed on certain Islamic practices.[9] Later in the Yuan period, as the Mongols became more sinicized, they tended to rely increasingly on Confucian-trained officials and much less on Muslims.[10]

In the wider Asian Islamic world, the Yuan had an indirect but obvious influence. The conquest era itself had rendered overland caravans temporarily risky and therefore some trade had shifted to maritime routes. Compensating repercussions were felt as far away as the Red Sea and Cairo. Once in power, the Yuan were amenable to long-distance trade and relied heavily on the Muslim officials and merchants both along the overland routes and in their southern ports. This situation provided a stimulus to Muslim trade in much the same way as Tang commercial contacts with the Abbasids had done back in the ninth century and Song exportation had done in the late tenth through twelfth centuries. Although warfare among the branches of the Mongol ruling family continued to put the caravan routes at risk periodically, generally there was more overland contact than before.

In West Asia, the branch of the Mongols known as the Il-khans (vicerulers) defeated the Saljuqs and conquered extensively until they were stopped in 1260 in Syria. They left a wide path of death, destruction, and altered demographics. The last Abbasid caliph in Baghdad was executed in 1258, and the caliphate reemerged only as a puppet office away from the Mongols, in Egypt. As they settled down to rule, most directly in Iran, the Il-khans indicated their preference for land-based power by choosing inland capital cities such as Tabriz and Qazwin. They were never able to expand their control as far as the Mediterranean, and they appeared relatively uninterested in the Persian Gulf.

The Il-khans found in Iran, as the Yuan had in China, a level of civilization higher than their own. Contact with Islam was not new. Even before the time of Chinggis Khan, the tribes of the Mongol confederacy had established contact with the Muslim merchants of Central Asia, who brought them the grain and horses they needed. A European visitor to the Mongolian capital of Karakorum in 1254, after expansion was well under way, found a Muslim quarter in that city.[11] In Iran, the Mongols found themselves living within a Muslim context. The Il-khans eventually chose to convert to the religion of their subjects and to patronize Persian Islamic high culture, in contrast to the Yuan, who remained somewhat aloof from things Chinese.

The Mongols did not rule for long across Asia. Sedentarization seemed to sap their vigor. They were unable to deal effectively with internal competition for power, and those who succeeded Chinggis Khan, based in Beijing, lost their clout beyond China. In about 1340, the Il-khans in Iran suffered internal political failure. At nearly the same time—no more than a decade later—the population of Iran was decimated by the Black Death, the plague for which the Mongols themselves had probably been the carriers.[12] The Il-khans were able to bequeath to their successors only their military prestige, which was relatively undiminished. The best known of these successors was the Muslim ruler Timur (Temür the Lame), who established a huge but ephemeral military empire in Central Asia and Iran, in conscious imitation of the early Mongols. Timur butchered and plundered, and he ruled by occupational force rather than institutional administration, something the Il-khans had at least attempted to do.[13] After his death in 1405, his regime collapsed in fewer than fifty years. Timur, perhaps better than anyone, illustrates the military state taken to an extreme. Meanwhile, the Mongol Yuan were defeated by the Chinese Ming in 1368, about three decades after the Il-khans had faded from power. (Only the Russian Mongol khanate of Kipchak, also known as the Golden Horde, persisted much longer.) One result of the general collapse of Mongol power was that the cross-Asian routes lost once again their relative security. This situation in turn contributed to a further shift of trade toward maritime routes, a shift begun during the Mongol conquests. So, imbedded in land-based history was a stimulus to the maritime expansion in which Muslims would excel.

Ayyubids and Mamluks

In the late eleventh century, well before the Mongol-Timurid era in Iran, Turkic Saljuq princes ruled northern Syria and Asia Minor. The Fatimids, weakened by drought and internal dynastic disputes, were still in power in Egypt and sometimes they extended influence into southern geographic Syria, or Palestine. At the very end of the century, the First Crusade reached the region. The presence of European enemies provided a common external threat and helped to bring about political reorganization in Syria and Egypt. This reorganization was accomplished by two successive regimes that ruled from Cairo, the Ayyubids and the Mamluks (Map 3.2). While many of the personnel of these regimes were Central Asian, they were not migrant conquerors but either slaves or mercenaries. Their administrations were not modeled directly on the Central Asian tribal tradition but rather were extensions of the military-slave system developed in the ninth century by the Abbasids; they were, therefore, distinct in origin but similar to the military patronage state.

First came a short-lived dynasty, the Ayyubids, founded by a hero of the Crusader era, the Kurdish mercenary Salah al-din ibn Ayyub (Saladin), who was powerful from about 1170 until his death in 1192. Both an able military commander and an astute politician, he managed to usurp the Isma'ili Fatimid throne and bring Egypt back into the fold of Sunni Islam. He mustered a slave-based army and also acquired a modest naval fleet of about eighty vessels, which he used to fend off the third wave of Crusaders.[14] Despite his successes, Saladin did not initiate a stable dynasty. When the Ayyubid family later succumbed to infighting, in about 1250, it was replaced by its own army, cavalry slave-soldiers who were acquired from Turkic Central Asia and later from the Caucasus region. This new regime took its name from the personal status of its recruits, that is, *mamluk,* an Arabic word meaning "slave" or "owned." The regime dealt effectively not only with its former masters but also with the Crusaders and the Mongols. The Mamluks, under a general called Baybars, deflected the Mongols from Syria in 1260 at Ayn Jalut. This battle marked the first time that the Mongols had been defeated in the Middle East, and from it the Mamluks derived much of the military legitimacy they needed to rule. They were a foreign elite, ruling over and patronizing the culture of the Arab Islamic heartland, just as the Il-khans were foreign rulers in the Persian Islamic cultural zone. The two regimes coexisted uneasily for about a century. Long after the Mongol collapse, the Mamluks continued in power, until 1517. Their longevity had much to do with their successful transformation of the military-slave system into a governing institution. Their eventual failure had much to do with their unwillingness to use firearms or to build a strong navy.

The maritime history of the Mamluks begins with a naval exploit ordered by Baybars, the hero of Ayn Jalut. After defeating the Mongols, he had consolidated his position as sultan. In 1270, he ordered a maritime expedition against Cyprus. His vessels were manned not by landlubber Mamluks but by local sailors. The results were disastrous, indicating a substantial decline in Muslim Mediterranean naval power since the heyday of the Fatimids. Baybars wrote to the king of Cyprus, minimizing the

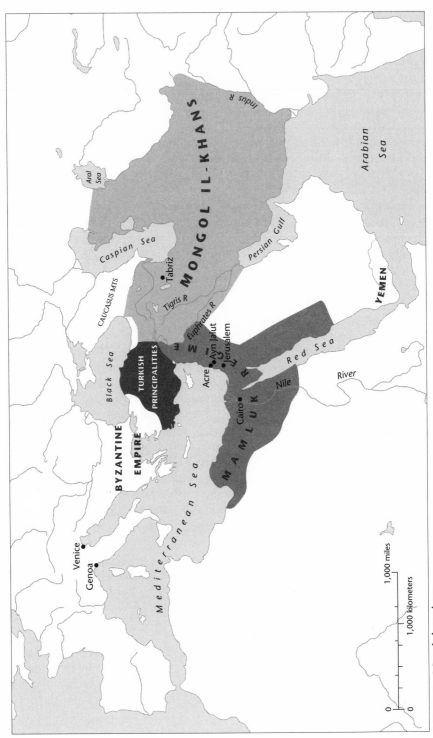

MAP 3.2 Mamluk regime

recent maritime loss in relation to his unquestionable success as a cavalry commander on land. He commented to the king, "Your horses are ships, while our ships are horses."[15] The Mamluks never built a permanent navy and in fact destroyed port facilities along the greater Syrian coast so that they could not be used by European enemies.[16]

Yet, despite a steppe backgound, the Mamluks did not close their eyes to the sea. They had inherited the maritime commercial networks of Fatimid Cairo and realized that revenues generated from that trade were crucial to their own prosperity. They maintained port facilities on the Egyptian coasts of the Mediterranean and Red Sea, which saw an increase in trade volume after the collapse of the Mongols.[17] These ruling Mamluks did not go to sea themselves as merchants but clearly had the incentive to invest in trade and take an interest in its conduct.

Evidence for Mamluk involvement in maritime trade is varied. One type of information comes from the work of S.D. Goitein, who analyzed a large cache of commercial documents and letters originally found in two medieval Jewish genizas in Cairo and now spread out in several European and U.S. libraries. (A geniza was a room or other space for depositing papers which could not be destroyed because the name of God appeared on them.) Goitein pieced together an impressive history of Jewish trade, which stretched into the Indian Ocean as well as the Mediterranean and from which a picture of sophisticated, wide-ranging Egyptian trade in general can be extrapolated.[18]

There is other, sketchy evidence about a group of wholesale merchants called the Karimis, who date back to late Fatimid times.[19] They were cosmopolitan and most if not all were Muslim. Handling the flow of Asian pepper and spices through Egypt toward Europe was crucial to their success. The Karimis sailed in convoy through the Red Sea to and from western Indian ports, such as Calicut and Quilon (Kawlam). They apparently received official protection during both the Fatimid and Mamluk eras. It may be that Cairo administrations protected the Karimis in order to help maximize their profits, which in turn made possible the exaction of heavy taxes. Around the turn of the fifteenth century, the agrarian economy of Egypt deteriorated; probably to compensate for this loss, the Mamluk rulers became more directly interested in maritime trade. In 1429, a Mamluk sultan named Barsbay—not to be confused with Baybars, mentioned previously—tried to monopolize the import and reexport of pepper.[20] He may have intended only to restrict European access to the valuable commodity, but he may also have wanted to break the economic power of the Karimis in favor of his own clique. Whatever his intentions, the sultan and the Karimis wound up in conflict. The Karimis wanted to continue to trade directly with Europeans and resisted central efforts to stop them. The outcome is not entirely clear. One interpretation is that the Karimis lost the struggle with their ruler and disappeared within about fifty years. The broader contention in this case is that the arbitrary interference of the central regime damaged the commercial economy, rendering Egypt vulnerable to the Venetians.[21] A similar view stresses the negative effects on Egypt of competition from the Yemen and western Arabia.[22] A third, quite different, opinion holds that the sultan failed to break the Karimi monopoly and that the group did not completely disappear. Furthermore, according to this view, the Karimis' general decline might be better explained by the impact of the fourteenth century plague on the merchant community.[23] The issue of the decline of the Karimis has yet to be resolved to everyone's satisfaction.

Another type of evidence concerning Mamluk interest in maritime trade can be derived from the ambivalent relationship that the Mamluks had with Venice. At the same time that the slave-soldiers gained control of the Syrian coast (e.g., of Acre in 1291), Venice was turning its attention toward Syria and Egypt. The Venetian motive was to avoid strong competition from Byzantines and Genoese in the Black Sea region. The Mamluks and Venetians, therefore, shared a common interest in trade.[24] This relationship persisted into the very early sixteenth century even though the Mamluks consistently blocked the Venetians from the Red Sea and, under Barsbay, restricted their access to pepper.

The Mamluks certainly did not establish a sea-borne empire, but they were the clearest exception to the apparent general rule of this era that Islamic military states took only marginal official interest in maritime concerns. The Fatimid maritime legacy, shifts in trade due to Mongol disruptions, and the constant factor of Egypt's geographic location were responsible for the exceptional situation.

The Delhi Sultanate

Beyond the Middle East, in northern India, the military state was represented by the Delhi Sultanate, which consisted of several successive dynasties ruling between 1206 and 1526, long past the Mongol era. The distinct ruling groups were the Ghurids (also known as a slave or mamluk dynasty), Khaljis, Tughluqs, Sayyids, and Lodis. They were all Turkic except the Lodis, who were Afghani; they represented various combinations of the Central Asian military patronage state and the Middle Eastern Islamic military-slave system. The early sultans had difficulty holding northern India together, but they were able to withstand Mongol raids in the thirteenth century. These Turkic and Afghani rulers, although not necessarily pious, were patrons of the Persian Islam they had adopted before coming to India. Many artisans and intellectuals who fled conflicts elsewhere in the Islamic world sought safety and patronage in Delhi. By the end of the thirteenth century, Delhi was a major urban center of Islamic culture dominated by a foreign minority. Despite cultural vitality and an impresssive military reputation, the sultanate suffered, by the fourteenth century, the negative effects of regional rebellion and inadequate administration. The Deccan province broke away under the rule of another Muslim regime, the Bahmanis. The Tughluqs were not able to stop destructive raids by Timur at the end of the century, and the sultanate declined precipitously after that.

The maritime history of the Delhi Sultanate is limited, probably because the internal economy of northern India was fairly self-sufficient and there was no compelling need to control maritime ports. The large province of Bengal and its ports were, more often than not, controlled by separatist governors or independent rulers. However, the second regime at Delhi, the Khaljis, seized the western coastal province of Gujarat in about 1303 with the intention of skimming the lucrative trade revenues of its ports, especially Cambay. As a result of Khalji intervention, Muslim commercial influence grew in the coastal region, and presumably customs revenues benefited the central administration as well. Shortly after Timur sacked Delhi in 1398, Gujarat was able to assert its independence and formed a separate government as a minor sultanate.[25] Despite the political change, Muslim merchants in the Gujarati ports continued to thrive, as did their Hindu counterparts.

During much of the Sultanate era, the south was closed to Muslim military and political expansion by the Hindu kingdom of Vijayanagar, in power from 1336 to 1565, which competed vigorously with both Delhi and the Bahmani state. Like the north, the south enjoyed a fairly self-sufficient internal economy. In the past, beginning in the eighth century, commerce had been organized by Hindu merchants through large guilds. For unclear reasons, possibly including the impact of Muslim-controlled trade, these merchant guilds declined in the thirteenth century and finally disappeared by 1500. For the Vijayanagar period, most exports and the very few imports (e.g., horses needed for the cavalry) found their way out of or into southern India by way of independent Hindu, Jain, and especially Muslim merchants on the coasts.[26] Neither the Delhi Sultanate nor Vijayanagar was a maritime power.

Early Ottomans

The military state was manifested by yet another group, the Turkic Ottomans from Central Asia, who had earlier settled in Asia Minor and who eventually conquered both the local Saljuq state and the neighboring Byzantines, beginning in the late thirteenth century. A major achievement of the Ottomans was to combine the strength of the military state with the longevity of an effective bureaucracy, the latter learned from Abbasid and Byzantine traditions. The Ottomans did become a naval power, especially in the Mediterranean.

The Ottoman tribal state crossed the symbolic threshold of empire in 1453 with the conquest of the Byzantine capital, Constantinople, or Istanbul. The internally weakened state of the Byzantines left the door open for an anticlimactic Turkish victory, but the conquest appeared to be a watershed. It certainly had profound psychological repercussions. Europeans feared unstoppable Islamic imperialism. Muslims were heartened by the victory, which appeared to compensate for losses of territory and strength in Muslim Spain during the early *reconquista*. A few decades later, the Portuguese found their way around Africa to the Indian Ocean, marking the start of a European effort to bypass overland Asian routes controlled by Islamic regimes, notably the Mamluks and Ottomans. In time, this maritime advance would overshadow the Turkish conquest of Constantinople.

The few significant Ottoman naval engagements of the fifteenth century were fought with the Venetians over control of certain ports and islands in the Mediterranean. The Ottomans did not muster significant naval power until the turn of the sixteenth century, a period covered in the next chapter. Naval and commercial maritime strength became increasingly important to the Ottomans in their competition with the Hapsburgs of central Europe and in their sixteenth-century commercial ventures. In the Indian Ocean region, to which they gained access through the Red Sea and Persian Gulf, the Ottomans would also make important efforts.

Clearly, the major Muslim powers between 1050 and 1500 were land-based and more interested in armies than in navies. In northern India, the Delhi Sultanate derived its most dependable revenues from agricultural production and taxation. Muslim and Hindu South Asia had a wide variety of resources and commodities available on a local or regional basis, making self-sufficiency a possibility. In turn, the expectation of self-sufficiency reduced the impulse toward long-distance maritime trade. In more arid, less populous, and less productive West Asia, the economy was far more dependent on the caravan trade that reflected the region's geographic middleman position between the rest of Asia and Europe. The regimes of Egypt, well-positioned between the Mediterranean and the Red Sea, took an active if not necessarily helpful interest in the affairs of their seafaring merchants, which was exceptional. The more usual lack of centralized imperial intervention did not, however, inhibit the maritime expansion of Islam and its trade. The restrictions on access to power within the foreign military regimes may have encouraged independent action by merchants.

Maritime Growth and Expansion: Western India, East Africa, and Especially Southeast Asia

Maritime Muslims gained a high profile in western India during the eleventh through fifteenth centuries. Not only did the existing Muslim merchant communities grow—through birthrate, conversion, and new immigration—but also those same communities participated in expansion into East Africa and Southeast Asia (Map 3.3).[27] They remained culturally and politically distinct from the Delhi Sultanate.

The success of foreign Muslim merchants at ports along India's west coast attracted the participation of Indian converts. The religious identities of these coastal merchant communities were not monolithic. The majority, those of the Sunni branch of Islam, tended to follow the Shafi'i school of law, then common in Arabia. (This practice was a point of contrast with the Delhi Sultanate, in which the Hanafi school prevailed.) Those of the Shi'i persuasian were often Isma'ili, belonging to either of two subsects dating back to an eleventh-century Fatimid dispute. One group, the Bohras, had ties to the Isma'ili minority in the Yemen; the name of this group derives from a Gujarati word for merchant.[28] The other group, the Khojas, incorporated Hindu practices and symbols and thereby established an Indian form of Islam.[29] Shafi'is, Bohras, and Khojas tended to conduct business within their own groups, but in relation to Hindus, they constituted a Muslim bloc.

Territorial power generally remained in the hands of Hindu rulers, while the sea was the dominion of the predominantly Muslim merchant community.[30] There were some cases, among both Hindus and Muslims, of merchants who occupied leadership positions in the military or in politics.[31] Coastal Muslims remained in enclaves, since they did not fit into the Hindu caste system, but there are examples of Muslims accommodating to a Hindu environment, e.g., abstaining from beef, paying taxes, and serving in the army of a Hindu ruler.[32] Often Muslim merchants came to play an indirect political role, as was the case in Calicut, where the Hindu ruler, called a *zamorin,* recognized a need to consider maritime interests in policy decisions. In many ports with large Muslim communities, origin myths evolved, providing Islamic legitimacy for economic and/or political power.[33] The myths usually linked the dominant Muslims directly to Arabia and to the Prophet Muhammad's family or tribe and not to the Turks and Afghanis of the Delhi Sultanate.

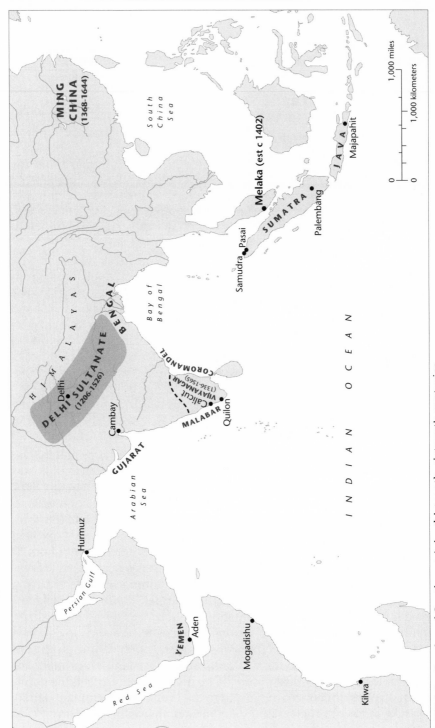

MAP 3.3   South and Southeast Asia, thirteenth–sixteenth centuries

We have explicit evidence of the vitality of western Indian trade from the famous North African Muslim traveler Ibn Battuta. He visited several western Indian ports in the mid-fourteenth century and attested to the significance of Muslim enclaves, particularly at Cambay in the Gujarati region. Ibn Battuta noted vessels owned by the sultan of Delhi that operated from Cambay and Calicut but observed that the majority of vessels were neither royal nor official. The foreign Muslims he saw came from Bahrain, Iraq, Oman, the landlocked Iranian city of Qazwin, and other distant points. The Chinese were well represented. Ibn Battuta reported thirteen junks at the port of Calicut, which dwarfed the local craft. He knew of Chinese merchants in residence at Quilon, some of whom may have been Muslim.[34] There were indigenous converts to Islam as well, notably the Shafi'i Mappilas of the region of Malabar, roughly modern Kerala. One of their rulers was the Hindu zamorin of Calicut. The Mappilas supplied export products, such as pepper and ginger, to the Malabari ports frequented by Middle Eastern Muslim merchants.[35]

From both western India and the Middle East, Muslim maritime merchants expanded outward. Some may have been seeking more political control over trade. A few reasons for the *extent* of this often private activity can be suggested. Merchants would go far out of their way, for example, (1) when barriers limited growth within their usual bounds and/or (2) when opportunities for profit at a distance balanced or exceeded the extra cost and risk of traveling farther. Navigation and ship technology had to be up to the challenge.

East Africa

The monsoons had always made central East Africa a possible destination for vessels from the littorals of the Red Sea, Persian Gulf, and Arabian Sea; certainly trade among Arabia, western India, and East Africa had been going on long before the rise of Islam. By the eleventh century, improvements in vessels made such contact easier, more profitable, and therefore attractive to more people. In terms of settlement, there had been a trickle of south Arabian and other Muslim migrants from at least the tenth century. The settlements grew in number and size during the thirteenth through fifteenth centuries, and that particular timing requires an explanation. Documentation is scarce, but it seems likely that political conditions elsewhere prompted relocation. There is some evidence, for example, that a group of settlers from Tashkent in Central Asia, fleeing the Mongol onslaught in the thirteenth century, moved to Mogadishu on the southern edge of East Africa's horn in what is now Somalia.[36] Another example is the prominent merchant family called the Mahdalis, from the Yemen. Fierce and sometimes violent competition over Red Sea trade between the Mamluks and an independent dynasty of the Yemen (the Rasulids, 1220s–1454) may have caused the Mahdalis to move to the East African island of Kilwa, where they already had commercial connections. They arrived at the turn of the fourteenth century and soon after imposed themselves as rulers of the island.[37]

The reasons for emigration away from unfavorable conditions are all rather speculative. It is possible also to suggest the attractions of East Africa for settlement. In comparison to much of the coast along the Red Sea, Persian Gulf, and northern Arabian Sea, much of East Africa was fertile and well watered.[38] In the fourteenth century, there was an increase in the world demand for gold, which could be obtained from Zimbabwe.[39] Other exports included ivory, mangrove poles (used, for example, in Arabian houses), as well as slaves from the interior. It is impossible to give accurate numbers of foreign settlers or African converts, but clearly much of coastal East Africa was drawn into the Islamic maritime sphere after 1200. By the end of the fifteenth century, there were between thirty and forty independent coastal towns that had been founded by immigrant Muslims.[40] In addition to the appearance of mosques, the construction of a fourteenth-century palace complex, called Husuni Kubwa, by a Mahdali ruler of Kilwa, is an indication of the extent and permanence of Muslim dominance there.

Southeast Asia

A few Arab merchants probably made their way to Southeast Asia before the rise of Islam. Arab *Muslim* enclaves existed in Southeast Asia by at least the eighth century, and some of the foreign Muslims expelled from Canton in 879 resettled there. As early as the eleventh century, there was foreign sufi missionary activity, but it was not until after 1300 that much conversion took place, mainly to Shafi'i Islam.[41] By then, Islamization was well under way along the coasts of India, and it was Indian Muslims who, following in the path of their Hindu and Buddhist predecessors, traveled in considerable numbers to Southeast Asia, where some settled. Technology was already sufficient for this regular, sustained contact. An important example is the Chinese floating compass, adopted by Muslim sailors in the 1200s; this compass, as opposed to the sextant, made it possible to navigate even when stars were not visible.[42] At first, Indian Muslims established themselves in Java and Sumatra. Later, Indian and Southeast Asian Muslims would carry their commodities and Islam to the Malay peninsula, then to Brunei on Borneo, to the Celebes (Sulawesi) and the Maluku spice islands, and finally to southern Mindanao in the Philippines.

The initial Muslim expansion in Southeast Asia roughly coincides with Eurasian recovery from the fourteenth-century plague and an increase in population and consumer demand for goods, including spices and pepper. The timing of the expansion also encourages the assumption that the relative instability of cross-Asian caravan routes after the decline of the Mongols was a factor. Caravans were still a major mode of transportation, but sea routes now seemed safer and therefore increasingly attractive. This shift might have occurred anyway, due to the increase in the size—and therefore cargo capacity—of Asian ships, especially those built in China, a circumstance which reduced the relative cost of maritime transportation and allowed more trade in bulk commodities.[43] At the very least, however, the Mongol collapse hastened the process. The Ming dynasty, which displaced the Mongol Yuan in 1368, provides a further explanation. The ethnically Chinese Ming had come to power on a wave of anti-"barbarian" sentiment, and their official policies were typically restrictive about direct, "corrupting" foreign trade at China's ports. This obstacle meant that now it would be easier for foreign Muslim merchants to obtain Chinese goods in Southeast Asia, where Chinese merchants still regularly sailed.

Arguably, the emergence of Melaka (Malacca) on the Malay coast as a Muslim-dominated entrepôt was one of the most important events in Indian Ocean history in the fifteenth century.[44] By then, foreign Muslim enclaves dotted the northern shores of Sumatra and Java and posed a challenge to indigenous patterns of trade. The Hindu-Buddhist maritime state of Srivajaya was long gone. Its successor state, Majapahit, named for its principal port on Java, was weakened by the incursions of nearby Muslim forces. The regime also suffered a debilitating internal conflict at the turn of the fifteenth century. Although the final blow from Muslim competitors did not come until a century later, a weak Majapahit left a regional political vacuum in which piracy and maritime warfare flourished. In these unsettled conditions, Melaka emerged from fishing village status to that of a major entrepôt. The story goes that the founder was a dispossessed Hindu prince named Parameshwara, said to be from the Majapahit ruling family by marriage but originally from Malay royalty. He sought his fortune away from his rivals and wound up at Melaka, where he recognized the potential of its excellent natural harbor and strategic position. To the port, he enticed a number of merchant acquaintances from Palembang on Sumatra. He was so successful in this enterprise that the regional balance of commercial power shifted noticeably in his favor. He was, however, still vulnerable enough that he had to strive to maintain good relations with the Hindu and Muslim ports and

Chinese settlements on Java and Sumatra, and he briefly paid tribute to a new Thai kingdom on the mainland. Parameshwara made a marriage alliance with the Muslim-dominated port of Pasai (Pasé) on Sumatra, which strengthened Melaka's position in relation to Hindu ports of the region. The proselytizing sultan of Pasai demanded that the Melakan ruler—Parameshwara in his old age or possibly his son—become Muslim, which he did in about 1420.[45] A seventeenth-century court chronicle credits Melaka's commercial success to this conversion.[46] Melaka was drawn into the developing Muslim Indian Ocean networks.

This transformation of a fishing village into a Muslim entrepôt took place at about the same time that the Ming regime in China, under the emperor Chengzu, sent out a series of large naval expeditions, beginning in 1405, the unclear purposes of which apparently included both commerce and political show of force. The Ming may have been particularly interested in suppressing piracy, which, since the decline of Majapahit, had been hurting China's trade in the Southeast Asian region. The commander of most of these expeditions was the Grand Eunuch, a Muslim named Zheng He, who possibly wanted either to link China to the growing Muslim maritime networks or to compete with them. The expeditions reached as far as Aden, Hurmuz, and the East African coast, but contact was perhaps best sustained at Melaka, which sent tributary missions to China and, in return, enjoyed the leverage of Chinese protection against regional competitors.[47] Parameshwara himself is said to have visited China three times between 1411 and 1419.[48] After 1433, China abruptly stopped its naval expeditions, partly because of military preoccupations in the north and partly because extensive maritime effort was viewed by a new emperor as too costly. The relationship between the rise of Melaka and the Zheng He expeditions remains poorly understood.

There is another view of the rise of Melaka, approached from the perspective of Southeast Asian history rather than from that of Islamic history. This view holds that Parameshwara's success was coincidental with the Ming expeditions and attracted Ming attention; Melaka became the preferred Southeast Asian port for the Chinese. This relationship weakened after the expeditions ended, and so to compensate, Melaka worked to become the major regional outlet for Javanese products. To do this, Melaka deliberately and successfully competed with Pasai and other ports for Sumatran pepper.[49] This explanation disregards the possibility of deliberate Muslim networking but is consistent with the contention that a prosperous Melaka was part of the Indian Ocean Muslim networks.

Melaka did not enjoy a developed hinterland, and so its economy was dependent on maritime commerce. Trade policies were designed in order to attract the maximum volume of trade. The Melakan government existed for the purpose of directing a commercial enterprise. The ruling family built up a navy to suppress piracy and acquired Southeast Asian slaves as crews and dockworkers.[50] The government also set attractive duty rates. Sometimes doing so meant deviating from Islamic commercial law, which stipulated the most favorable terms for fellow Muslims. The Portuguese observer Tomé Pires, in his *Suma Oriental,* suggests that customs duties were assigned in order to encourage the carrying trade. The rates were on the attractvely low side compared with those of other Southeast Asian ports, particularly those of the mainland.[51]

The deliberate policies at Melaka worked. It became a thriving entrepôt with a population estimated anywhere from 50,000 to a rather high 200,000—in any case, of significant size for the region.[52] A large percentage of merchants who regularly visited the port or who were resident there were South Asians from Gujarat, Bengal, and the Coromandel coast. Of these, most were Muslim. There were also numerous Javanese, most of whom were Muslim, and Chinese, some of whom were also converts to Islam.[53] Among all these foreigners, Gujaratis were most influential. Tomé Pires remarks that Melaka and the Gujarati port of Cambay were mutually dependent on each other for their prosperity.[54] He may overstate Cambay's dependence on Melaka somewhat, since Cambay was a larger port and the hub of a wide-reaching, complex trade pattern.[55] However, the primary commodities of exchange between the two ports were certainly critical to the success of both: Southeast Asian pepper and Gujarati cotton. Javanese and Sumatran ports lost their former place in long-distance trade and became dependent on Melaka as the only major outlet for pepper and rice produced on the islands.[56]

The depth and orthodoxy of Melaka's Islam have often been questioned. The apparently pragmatic conversion of the Melakan ruler, the continued observance of animistic and Hindu traditions, and the divergence from Islamic commercial law all suggest qualifications.[57] Also, Melaka shared with many port towns a reputation for rough behavior. Perhaps the harshest assessment came from an accomplished Arab Muslim pilot, Ibn Majid, who recorded his impressions of the port's inhabitants in the 1480s:

> They have no culture at all. ... You do not know whether they are Muslim or not. ... They are thieves for theft is rife among them and they do not mind. ... They appear liars and deceivers in trade and labor.[58]

But the Islamic link was important. As in several South Asian ports, an Islamic foundation myth evolved at Melaka to legitimize the rulers. Also, when the port was in decline near the turn of the sixteenth century, rendering it vulnerable to the warships of Java and later to those of the Portuguese, the last Melakan sultan appealed to Islam by trying to make his port a place of pilgrimage.[59]

A Note on Arabization and Islamization

Everywhere that Muslim merchants and missionaries settled in coastal South Asia, East Africa, and Southeast Asia, conversion was followed by permanent Islamization, often measured by the presence of Muslim legal and educational instititutions. Neither the spread of Islam nor that of the Arabic language was as pervasive as it had been in the Middle East and North Africa as a result of the early Arabian conquests. The later, distant Islamization was qualified by the persistence of local culture and traditions and, in some cases, by the minority status of Muslims. Arabization also varied. Converts took Arab names but not Arab tribal affiliations, as many early converts in the Middle East had done. Arabic had an important but not overwhelming impact. In coastal South Asia, Arabic vocabulary made some inroads beyond religious usage. However, both Sanskritic Gujarati and Dravidian Malayalam, used by Hindus and Muslims alike, kept their linguistic integrity. In East Africa, Arab settlers strongly influenced the unwritten local Bantu language and its dialects. A new language emerged called Kiswahili. Much later, when Kiswahili came to be written, the Arabic script was employed. (The first preserved literature dates from the eighteenth century.) In Southeast Asia, Arabic also influenced both vocabulary and script and brought some commonality to the languages of the Malay peninsula, Sumatra, and Java.[60]

An Assessment of Asian Commerce in the Middle Era

There is a growing body of literature which insists that before the Europeans arrived in Asia in the sixteenth century, Asians had enjoyed a long period of relatively peaceful, lucrative, and unrestricted trade, an argument that is open, we will see, to some dispute. The argument continues, more convincingly, that the organization and financing of this trade was at least as sophisticated as the maritime commerce of contemporary Europeans, most of whom were still confined largely to the Mediterranean.[61] One contributor to this general view is Janet Abu-Lughod. She has suggested a Eurasian "world system"—that is, a large though not truly global economic interchange—existing between the mid-thirteenth and mid-fourteenth centuries. This system linked Asia by land and sea with Europe. The individual circuits of the system consisted of trade regions which overlapped, making it possible, for example, for Chinese goods to reach Venice without a direct contact between the two.[62] Mongol control of much of Asia between 1250 and 1350 is a factor in Abu-Lughod's analysis; an oblong region encompassing the cross-Asian caravan routes controlled by the Mongols is one of her designated circuits. The *Pax Mongolica* facilitated the overland component of Eurasian trade, although it should be pointed out that this period of general stability lasted for only a brief time and had significant exceptions.[63] The system was not hierarchically arranged but rather was balanced, meaning that no one political power dominated it, no one core city or area drew to itself the lion's share of economic benefit. This balance also meant that no single culture or ideology characterized it. (Abu-Lughod partially undermines this last contention by emphasizing—correctly— the role played by *Muslims*.[64]) By arguing for the existence of a largely Asian thirteenth-century world system, Abu-Lughod challenges received opinion. A widely held view is that the *first* world system began to emerge in the fifteenth century, based in Europe; it preceded the emergence of industrial capitalism, through which a few European economic core cities peripheralized much of Asia and the Americas. This interpretation is associated with Fernand Braudel and Immanuel Wallerstein.[65] Abu-Lughod argues that the European-based system was not the only historically possible outcome in the past or, for that matter, in the future.[66] Her open, non-hierarchic system with multiple core areas might, she thinks, be an alternate model should the present capitalist world system ever collapse.

While the thirteenth-century system might survive as an abstract model, its actual history was short. The circuits of the system were, according to Abu-Lughod, seriously damaged in the fourteenth century. The elements of her explanation for this damage have already been introduced: the fourteenth-century plague, the collapse of the Mongols, the weakening of the Delhi Sultanate, and the closure of China. The plague decimated not only the Mongols who carried it but also the populations of distant regions, including Mamluk Egypt and the Italian city-states, all vital to the system. Also, the political collapse of the Mongols meant the breakdown of the long-distance caravan routes and a disruption of land-based political stability. The Delhi Sultanate, weakened internally by this time, was unable to resist Timur: Delhi was sacked in 1398 and never fully recovered until well into the Mughal era. The Ming of China, who had removed the Yuan in 1368, chose to regulate coastal trade closely, with the result that the volume of foreign trade at Chinese ports fell. All these factors together, argues Abu-Lughod, weakened Asian commerce and overall economy, a problem that could not be overcome in the period of time before the Europeans arrived. While Abu-Lughod does not address the issue, it can be assumed that, in relation to her interpretation, the successful Asian Muslim expansions of the era, such as those in coastal India, Southeast Asia, and East Africa, were not great enough to counterbalance contemporary difficulties and were not an appropriate basis for closing the economic and technological gaps between Asia and western Europe that began to appear in the fifteenth century.

An interpretation with as large a sweep as that of Abu-Lughod's is bound to attract discussion, both on specifics and on the general thesis. One point has to do with the lack of political hegemony over the whole system. Immanuel Wallerstein has argued that while the whole system, as Abu-Lughod defines it, was free of political hegemony, the circuits themselves *were* associated with dominant regimes and *were* hierarchically ordered. In fact, Wallerstein would prefer to view Abu-Lughod's system as an overarching framework for a cluster of small systems roughly equivalent to her circuits.[67] Also, political hegemony over the whole system was rendered impractical in the era of sailing ships because of the monsoons affecting the critical Asian maritime components. Strong prevailing winds lasting for months at a time made frequent round-trip communication impossible; the timing of contact was determined by nature, not by military or political considerations, a circumstance learned later by the Portuguese.[68]

A second point is that more attention might be paid to China's role in the rise or decline of the system. China's economic revolution took place in the eleventh century, well before the exceptional Mongol conquests of the mid-thirteenth century, and the relationship between the two calls for more clarification.[69]

A third point is that the Eurasian system was not without flaws; it wasn't just bad timing and bad luck that rendered the world system defunct in the fourteenth century and left Asia vulnerable to Europeans in the sixteenth century. For example, while Mongol rule may have facilitated *overland* trade, it can be argued that the world system did not and perhaps could not secure regional *maritime* trade adequately. This distinction is significant because the Europeans would arrive later by sea. There is considerable evidence of coercion and piracy in the Indian Ocean, which must have led to large protection costs before, during, and after the century from 1250 to 1350. Since piracy is a controversial concept, the term requires a definition appropriate to the context in which it is being used. Piracy is meant here to include any seizure of merchant vessels or cargo, and often the holding of crew or passengers for ransom, with obvious economic motive but not necessarily with political motive. Such seizures usually proliferated in areas where there was instability or intense rivalry. This definition is intended to be broad enough to include state-sponsored acts. Piracy in the South China Sea and eastern Indian Ocean has already been mentioned as a likely stimulus to the Ming ex-

peditions. The west coast of India was notorious for maritime depreda-
tions both before and after the arrival of Europeans.[70] The Southeast
Asian maritime state of Srivijaya (sixth through thirteenth centuries)
maintained a monopoly over the trade route between India and China
by keeping armed ships in the Straits of Melaka and by exacting protection payments, thus using force to control trade in a manner presaging
the Portuguese.[71] The geniza documents, most of which date between
the twelfth and first half of the thirteenth century, suggest rampant piracy in both the Mediterranean and Red Sea.[72] Ibn Battuta informs us
that it was common in the mid-fourteenth century for ships in the Indian Ocean to sail in armed convoy and to carry archers or other soldiers
aboard.[73] Chinese vessels were also heavily armed: He mentions cross-
bow archers aboard junks who shot naptha missiles.[74] He himself was
the victim of pirates off the western coast of India.[75] Before 1500, Muslim
Melaka possessed thousands of firearms and also Chinese-style cannon,
which had been used on vessels since the thirteenth century.[76] Just how
serious a detriment protection costs might have been or to what degree
they might have affected Abu-Lughod's system are difficult to gauge, but
numerous failures to secure trade need to be considered. The image of
relatively peaceful maritime commerce before the arrival of the Portuguese, who came with cannon bolted to the decks of their sturdy ships,
must be modified somewhat, though, arguably, Asian trade before 1500
was *politically* more open than it would be after the Portuguese tried to
establish a national monopoly.

Conclusion

Abu-Lughod challenges an overly Eurocentric view of world systems.
Since the scope in this chapter is not, of course, her entire Eurasian system in a single century but Islamic maritime Asia between the eleventh
and fifteenth centuries, it is useful to assess the role of the Muslim trade
networks in relation to Asian maritime trade as a whole. For this middle
era, Muslims formed major networks of carriers *within* a complex economy that arguably generated a world system between 1250 and 1350.
Muslim merchants situated themselves among and between the suppli-
ers of slaves and ivory in East Africa, the producers of rice and cotton in
the predominantly Hindu interior of India, and the producers of silk,
porcelains, and steel in Confucian China. Among the land-based Asian
empires, only the Mamluks and the Ming had significant impacts—positive and negative—on maritime trade.

In the centuries under discussion, Muslims from various regions constituted maritime networks unified not by Islamic imperial dominance
but by smaller political units, by culture, and (theoretically) by com-

monality of law. Characterizing the networks as Muslim leads to an important final point about the relationship between Muslim trade and the spread of Islamic society. Clearly, patterns of conversion developed through commercial and social contacts with successful foreign Muslim merchants. In fact, the initial growth of the commercial networks was due largely if not exclusively to conversion. There were both pragmatic and religious dimensions to this phenomenon. Some historians emphasize the former, even suggesting that by converting, an Asian merchant could raise his credit rating.[77] Pragmatic value attached to assuming a Muslim name as a result of conversion.[78] There is also the case of Buddhist rulers of the Arakan coastal province of Burma who took Muslim names, presumably in the interests of commerce, but did not convert.[79] The late fifteenth-century Portuguese traveler Duarte Barbosa seemed to believe that commercial success motivated conversion at Melaka: "Many foreign Muslims having established their trade became so rich thereby that they turned the people of the land into Moors [Muslims] also."[80] (It might be noted, too, that apostasy from Islam was forbidden, technically punishable by death, and was, in any case, rare.) It is, however, difficult to maintain a narrow causal relationship between commercial considerations and Islamization. The South and West Asian Muslims who sailed to East Africa and Southeast Asia were merchants of faith. Whatever the initial rationale of converts, this era saw the permanent spread of Islamic society from Mogadishu to Melaka.

4 The Conduct of Asian Muslim Trade, Sixteenth Through Eighteenth Centuries

The period of Asian history from roughly 1500 to 1800, when Europeans made their appearance but before the heyday of their imperialism, has generated considerable debate, much of it rooted in ideology. Controversy has had the beneficial result of raising issues and drawing out considerable data that might otherwise have remained unexplored. The debate is not usually directed toward Islamic Asia, per se, but it encompasses Muslims in a context very important to them. This chapter and the next examine the period that has elicited such divergent approaches and premises, with the intention of identifying contributions from the scholarly debate that enhance an understanding of the Muslim role in Indian Ocean history. Chapter 5 will also ask if the different positions can be reconciled.

In 1974, a study titled *The Asian Trade Revolution of the Seventeenth Century: The East India Companies and the Decline of the Caravan Trade* by the Danish scholar Niels Steensgaard, was published.[1] This book represents an important historiographical position, namely that European presence in Asian commerce was revolutionary as early as the 1620s. Employing effective organization and methods, the English and Dutch East India Companies attracted sufficient trade away from land caravans to the sea route so that they disrupted long-distance overland Asian trade significantly, with secondary effects on regional and local trade. This analysis is consistent with a global interpretation of history associated with Immanuel Wallerstein, who argues that Asia was incorporated into a world-system between the sixteenth and nineteenth centuries, as modes of production in Asia became more specialized and interdependent, in response to European demand.[2]

In 1979, a collection of essays appeared titled *The Age of Partnership: Europeans in Asia Before Dominion,* edited by Blair Kling and M. N. Pearson.[3] Although this book was not intended to contrast specifically with Steensgaard's work, the title and tenor do reflect a very different historiographical position: before nineteenth-century imperialism, European impact on Asia was limited. Whether as individuals or as agents of trading companies, Europeans in Asia before 1800 did not cause alterations in Asian commerce significant enough to be categorized as revolutionary. While Europeans did have an impact on long-distance commerce to Europe, within Asia they had little choice but to blend into regional and local trade as best they could. Some achieved financial success while others were dismal failures. This "partnership" view is roughly consistent with a segment of Marxist historiography that remains skeptical of Wallerstein's ideas.[4] Supporters of this position argue that despotic governments prevented Asia from evolving from feudalism into capitalism, a necessary step on the way to socialism. Production and commerce remained essentially traditional until the nineteenth century, when *industrial, wage labor* capitalism developed sufficiently in Europe to require the exploitation of Asia's raw materials, as opposed to the importation of its manufactured goods. It is important to emphasize that these historiographical lines are not always sharply drawn.

The Early-Modern Empires

In the sixteenth and seventeenth centuries, three dynasties dominated the predominantly Muslim portions of Asia: the Sunni Ottomans, whose rule extended from Asia Minor into Eastern Europe and into the Arab Middle East; the Twelver Shi'i Safavids in Iran, rivals to the Ottomans during the sixteenth and seventeenth centuries; and the Mughals, who controlled much though never all of India. In Confucian China, the Manchu Qing dynasty replaced the Chinese Ming. While all four empires remained essentially land-based, they acted on an awareness of the maritime dimension of Eurasia more than their predecessors had.

Ottomans

The Ottoman empire was successful not only as a military state but also as an institutionalized government and society, although eventually the high degree of bureaucratization hindered necessary flexibility. There was central control over administration, land tenure, and the army. The Sunni Islam of the rulers was institutionalized by the state: Islamic education and law were put under the direction of an official called the *shaykh al-islam,* who was appointed by the sultan himself and who ranked nearly as high as the prime minister (grand vizir). Even popular institutions such as guilds and a few major sufi brotherhoods became associated with the state. During long Ottoman success, the empire's political thinkers had time to be self-reflective and elaborate upon an unsurprising explanation for the existence of the state. Simply put, their theory posited a secure, productive agrarian population which provided tax revenues to support an ever-enlarging military; the conquering military expanded the agrarian tax base and secured the environment to encourage taxable productivity. This circular theory itself was conceived as land-based.[5]

In the late fifteenth century, expansion proceeded by sea as well as by land, and the Ottomans engaged in naval conflict with Venice. The Ottomans and Venetians contested former Byzantine ports in the northeastern Mediterranean region. The Ottomans eventually won the sporadic contest, which lasted from 1463 to 1502, and took over some of the Venetian dependencies, such as Lepanto in Greece. During the rest of the sixteenth century, the Ottomans came to a maritime stalemate with the Austrian Hapsburg empire, with its capital in Vienna, another essentially land-based power. Also during the sixteenth century, the Ottomans expanded a system of commercial agreements that later had, for them, negative economic consequences. These were the famous capitulations, by which the Ottomans attempted, in part, to strengthen an alliance with France against the Hapsburgs. The French—and later other Europeans as well—gained trade and legal privileges at Ottoman ports. The arrangements were mutually beneficial until Europe's Industrial Revolution; after that, Europeans were able to take advantage of assured access to Ottoman markets for their less expensively produced goods, doing damage to the Ottoman balance of trade.

In 1516–1517, the Ottoman Sultan Selim I, called "the Grim," doubled his territory and enhanced his prestige with the conquest of the Mamluk Middle East, that is, Egypt and Syria as well as coastal North Africa and the Hijaz province of Arabia. With the takeover of the Hijaz province the sultan gained Islamic legitimacy by virtue of controlling the holy cities of Mecca and Madina; Selim and his successors could now lay claim to the caliphate, which had been nominal since the Mongol execution of the Abbasid caliph at Baghdad in 1258. The revival of the office entailed stretching its definition: the Turkic Ottoman family did not have the required genealogical tie to the Arabian tribe of the prophet, Muhammad, but they made do. At this point, just before Selim's death in 1520, the Ottoman Empire was perhaps at its zenith.

The inclusion of Mamluk territory enlarged the Ottoman coastline dramatically, and this development was not incidental. Maritime access had figured into the complex motivations for conquest in the first place. The Ottomans had for some time wished to redirect the lucrative trade of Egypt and Syria to Istanbul or, even better, to control Cairo directly. When the Mamluks showed signs of military vulnerability, Sultan Selim began his conquest. Also, the Ottomans were aware that the Portuguese had staked claims in the Indian Ocean and Persian Gulf and were attempting to gain access to the Red Sea. At an earlier point, the Ottomans had even lent shipbuilding assistance to the Mamluks, who were themselves trying to hold back the Portuguese. There was, therefore, in 1516–1517, a concurrent need to defend the prize of Cairene trade even as it was being won. In 1521, just after Selim's famous son, Sulayman, ascended the throne, an Ottoman naval officer and cartographer called Piri Re'is wrote a book outlining his extensive knowledge of the world's seas; from this perspective, he apparently saw dire economic consequences in the European advance, and so his book urged Sulayman to expel the Portuguese.[6] It was only with difficulty, and after seizing the Yemen for obvious strategic reasons, that the Ottomans could close the Red Sea to the Portuguese.

From about 1525 to 1640, the Ottomans vacillated between their efforts by sea and and those by land and also between efforts in Asia and in Europe. Even though the Portuguese remained a threat in the Persian Gulf, Sulayman chose a major land campaign, beginning in 1525–1526, into the heart of eastern Europe. This resulted in the conquest of Hungary, bringing the empire to its greatest geographic extent (Map 4.1). Only after that, in the 1530s, did the Ottomans return further if limited attention to the Gulf. There were a few Ottoman raids against the Portuguese in East Africa and western India; however, the pressing objectives were to counter the Portuguese on the strategically located island of Hurmuz, at the entrance to the Persian Gulf, and to compete with the rival Safavids. The Ottomans conquered northern Iraq from Safavid Iran and the southern portion from tenacious independent tribal shaykhs, until finally they reached the Gulf and curved around it to the port town of Kuwait. The Baghdad-Basra corridor of commerce had in the past been a valuable economic asset to the Islamic world, and there was a chance it could be again. Not since early Abbasid times had a single Islamic power been in a position to control the eastern Mediterranean Sea *and* Iraq, with its access to the Gulf. Over the next seventy years, Baghdad changed hands a few more times, and it fell more decisively to the Ottomans in 1638.

During the same decades, however, it had become increasingly difficult for the Ottomans to hold their own against the Europeans in the West, either commercially or in terms of naval strength. More specifically, the Ottomans had suffered a serious defeat in 1571 at the battle of Lepanto, when a significant portion of their fleet was destroyed by European forces. The sultan, by then Selim II, and his prime minister, Mehmet Sokollu, oversaw the rebuilding of the fleet; the Ottomans continued to be a world power but Central and Western Europe increasingly challenged them. Furthermore, the growing Russian Empire was pressing in on the Black Sea region. The Ottomans believed it necessary to concentrate their naval and other military resources in the north and

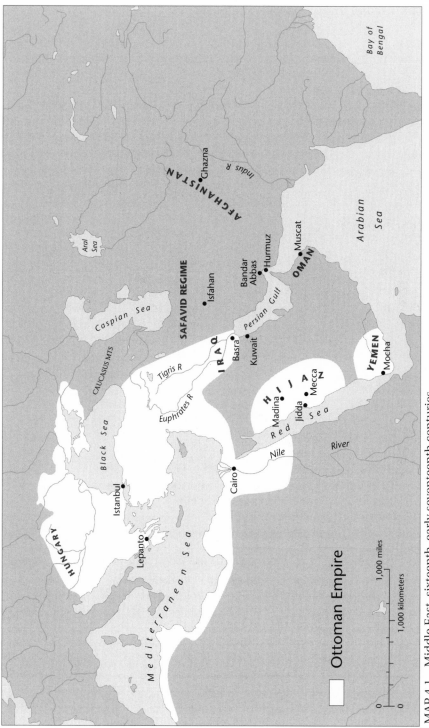

MAP 4.1   Middle East, sixteenth–early seventeenth centuries

west. Correspondingly, Ottoman naval and commercial activity diminished in the Indian Ocean region, although a number of individual merchants were Ottoman subjects. In the mid-eighteenth century, the rise in Arabia of tribal Muslim purists, the Wahhabis, challenged not only the religious legitimacy of the sultan but also residual Ottoman claims to the Persian Gulf and Arabian Sea.

With benefit of hindsight, one could argue that the Ottomans did not commit themselves sufficiently in the Gulf and Red Sea regions, that they may have lost an opportunity to build an Asian maritime empire. Another and not inconsistent view is that in 1526, with the initiation of a major campaign into Eastern Europe, the Ottoman regime made clear its decision to continue favoring land-based expansion, the traditional source of its strength.[7]

Safavids

The Safavids arose from a Turkic military state in northwestern Iran at the turn of the sixteenth century. They established their institutions with Iranian bureaucrats, who could call upon the Sasanid and Abbasid imperial traditions of the past and who also had available contemporary Ottoman models. Safavid institutions were less successful than those of the Ottomans partly because of tensions between a Turkic military and an Iranian administration.

The Safavids sharply differentiated themselves from the Sunni Ottomans, who were their principal territorial rivals, by imposing the Twelver Shi'i branch of Islam as their official ideology. The early Safavids arose from a mystical (sufi) order, the Safaviyya, popular among the Turkic tribesmen in northwestern Iran. The heterodox beliefs of the order included many ideas adapted from the Shi'i tradition. The founder of the dynasty, Isma'il, apparently decided that orthodox Shi'ism was preferable to his own eclectic, regional heterodoxy for the purposes of building an empire. There may have been an early expectation that Isma'il was the returned twelfth imam, but it was soon apparent that the Safavids were not going to fulfill messianic hopes.[8] In the absence of the twelfth imam, any government could only be imperfect; therefore, many of the Shi'i religious leaders, the ulama or mullas, remained aloof from the regime. Losing clear religious endorsement, the Safavid rulers relied more and more on the pre-Islamic Iranian past for legitimation. For example, they emphasized surviving ancient imperial symbols, such as the sun, the lion, and the title *shah* (king). Thus, an uneasy juxtaposition of ancient imperial and orthodox Shi'i traditions was established, even though the two rested on incompatible authorities. Unlike the Sunni Ottomans, who incorporated into their state Islamic institutions such as education and law, the Safavids failed to co-opt all the Shi'i leaders and the institutions they controlled as teachers and judges. Many of the mullas maintained grassroots ties and could influence public opinion against any actions of the Safavid or subsequent regimes which they construed as godless. The religious difference between the Ottomans and the Safavids did not much affect their respective commercial laws, but it did provide sanction for imperial competition that included commerce, such as the overland silk trade.

The Safavids competed with the Ottomans for control of Iraq and the region extending north into the Caucasus, including much of traditional Armenia and Kurdistan. Although they enjoyed initial victories, the Safavids were unable to hold all their territorial gains. The loss of Iraq during the 1530s, mentioned earlier in the Ottoman section, not only had economic consequences but also meant that Shi'i shrines in that region were now in Sunni Ottoman hands.[9] To the east, the Safavids reached an impasse against the Central Asian tribal state of the Uzbegs, and to the north they, like the Ottomans, soon had to worry about Russian imperial intentions. Although Twelver Shi'ism spread to eastern Arabian and island ports, the Persian Gulf did not provide an avenue for expansion because the Safavids lacked a naval force of any consequence.

Unable to expand their land-based state or its tax base, and at times blocked in the Persian Gulf by both the Ottomans established at Basra and the Portuguese, the Safavids had to be creative to retain power. It was the famous Shah Abbas, on the throne from 1588 until 1629, who gave his dynasty a new if short-lived lease on life by drawing Iran into international trade. Abbas made overtures to northern European states that had followed the Portuguese into the Gulf region. The English responded first, entering into a trade arrangement and agreeing to provide naval power to expel the Portuguese from the island of Hurmuz, which was accomplished in 1622. The Dutch and the French also made commercial agreements.[10]

What did Shah Abbas have to offer the northern Europeans? Initially, he held out the hope of concerted action against the Portuguese, a common enemy. Perhaps more important than any possible military cooperation, Abbas could offer a desirable commodity: silk. Shah Abbas monopolized the production and sale of silk in his realm and, therefore, was in a position to benefit from the high demand in Europe for raw silk and for cloth and rugs made from it.[11] By selling some of his silk to Europeans at his ports, Shah Abbas could both bypass Ottoman middlemen and increase Iran's share of the market in relation to the silk produced in Ottoman Syria. Some historians who see the Safavids as oriental despots tend to argue that in the long term, the high degree of economic centralization was damaging; but certainly in the short term, the trade revenues generated by Persian exports were a boon to the Safavid economy.[12] Isfahan became a well-financed showcase for Persian Islam, and a mainland entrepôt opposite the island of Hurmuz was renamed Bandar (port) Abbas, for the shah, and became a major commercial center.

Abbas's less capable successors soon left Iran open to fragmentation and invasion. They mismanaged revenues, failing to make necessary investments in irrigation and roads, so that the agrarian infrastructure began to erode. The hemmed-in and inactive military also began to degenerate. By 1722, when an Afghani tribal prince temporarily seized Isfahan, Safavid control had disintegrated, leaving the region to competing tribal groups. The most impressive competitor was Nadir Khan, who ruled southern Iran in the 1730s and 1740s and who took for himself the title of shah. Perhaps aware of the limits of his land-based power, he saw the value of a navy. He proceeded to buy, build, and capture vessels, which he manned with Arab crews, because his Persianized Turkic tribesmen lacked naval experience. The effort was insufficient. In 1740, a general mutiny occurred and many of the vessels found new owners on the Arab side of the Gulf. Nadir Shah tried to rebuild the force but was unable to achieve his maritime goal before his death in 1747.

Mughals

The Mughals, of Central Asian origin, established themselves in northern India between 1526 and 1556 (Map 4.2). While sometimes in conflict with the contemporary Safavids, the Mughals also maintained political and cultural ties with Iran through diplomacy and royal marriage. The name Mughal is a corruption of Mongol; the dynasty called itself Timuri, indicative of their claim to descent from the Mongols through Timur the Lame, who in turn had claimed to be a descendant of Chinggis Khan on his mother's side. The Mongol-Timuri geneological claims indicate a continued reliance on military prowess and prestige as the basis of rule. Like their predecessors of the Delhi Sultanate, the Mughals were a Persianized Muslim minority ruling over a vast Hindu majority. South Asian conversions did occur, often through the eclectic ministrations of sufi brotherhoods.

The Mughals were stronger militarily and administratively than any of the Delhi Sultans had been. The architect of the regime, Akbar, who ruled from 1556 to 1605, extended his military reach into part of the Deccan plateau of south central India. Akbar has been favorably compared with his near contemporaries the Ottoman Sultan Sulayman and the Safavid Shah Abbas. One of Akbar's achievements was to consolidate his new empire under a combination of military and administrative land-

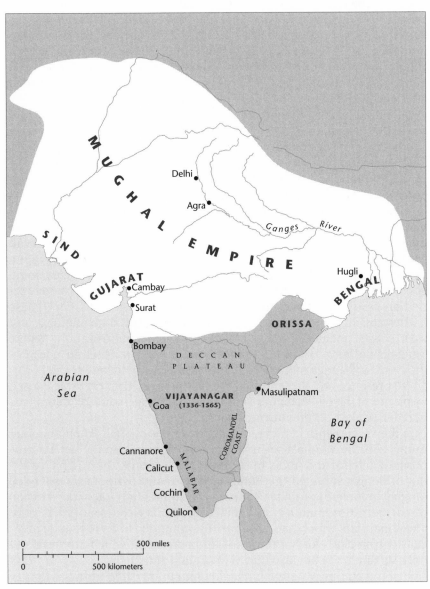

MAP 4.2   Mughal India, circa 1600

holdings which were to be regularly assessed for taxable value. The idea was to balance the army and the bureaucracy and give them both a vested interest in the stability of the central government. The land-based premise of power is unmistakable. Akbar also tried to overcome problems inherent in minority Islamic rule over Hindus by relaxing laws that burdened non-Muslims and by establishing a cult of his own, in which Hindu and other Indian traditions were grafted onto an Islamic core. Akbar's efforts to organize land and to achieve religious harmony eroded after his death in 1605.[13]

Under Akbar, the Mughals gained access to both the Arabian Sea and the Bay of Bengal. In 1573–1574, they took the sultanate of Gujarat, which had been independent of Delhi since about 1400. By the 1570s, Gujarat's main port, Cambay, was silting over; as a result, trade there shifted to the up-and-coming port of Surat to the south, which then became the major entrepôt of Mughal India. The huge province of Bengal, along with its ports that traded to the Coromandel coast, to Burmese and Thai ports, and to Southeast Asia, also came under Mughal dominance in 1576. The main effect of this coast-to-coast expansion was improved efficiency in getting inland products to ports, rather than the extension of the empire overseas.[14] Also, Akbar had additional roads built, which meant more goods traveled within the enlarged Mughal interior instead of being carried on vessels from port to port along India's coast.[15] The Portuguese had established themselves in various ports along both the east and west coasts, including areas beyond Mughal administration. Where Mughals did have coastal influence—for example at Hugli in Bengal— they took advantage of investment possibilities stimulated by the Portuguese presence but also endured the dampening effect on trade caused by pirates of mixed Portuguese and Asian parentage, some of whom harbored in Arakan on the Burmese coast.

In the seventeenth century, during the reigns of Shah Jahan and later Aurangzeb, the Mughals began to show more interest in the sea, for purposes of defense and trade. In the 1660s, for example, the Mughal governor of Bengal subdued the Eurasian pirates and temporarily extended Mughal influence to Arakan.[16] Aurangzeb conquered Golconda, a region of northern Coromandel, and gained temporary control over its port, Masulipatnam, which had become important due to its exchange of locally woven cloth for Southeast Asian pepper and which attracted not only Muslim trade but also that of the Dutch and English.[17] On the other side of the empire, where the major competition came from the fleet of the Hindu Marathas and marauders from Malabar ports, the number of Mughal ships at Surat rose from about fifty to over one hundred, and many of the new ones were large; also, an Arab mercenary fleet in the service of the Mughals was harbored just south of Bombay.[18] Rulers and officials invested in trade, welcomed Europeans at Surat, and tried to enrich public coffers through trade levies. However, unlike some of the smaller coastal polities who were dependent on sea trade, the Mughals had no ongoing maritime policy or strategy.[19]

Aurangzeb, also known as Alamgir, was the last powerful Mughal ruler (r. 1658 to 1707). In addition to his exploits mentioned earlier, which had direct maritime consequences, he also had to spend much of his time subduing regional rebels including Muslim Bengalis, Hindu Marathas in central India, and Sikhs in the Punjab. He also dealt with a tribal upsurge among the Rajputs and Jats of the northwest, an upsurge that continued beyond his reign, through the eighteenth century.[20] In an effort to stave off the collapse of centralized authority, he reimposed Islamic law on non-Muslims, which, instead of providing stability, contributed to the alienation of much of his subject population.

China

The other empire relevant to Asian maritime history during this era was China, which continued to defy its own isolationist image. Most economic growth was domestic: production within and trade among the regions of China increased. The Ming ruled until 1644 and were replaced by the Manchu Qing dynasty, which lasted until the early twentieth cenutry. There were two expansionist phases of foreign trade.[21] The first phase occurred between 1590 and 1620, in the late Ming era, and appears to have been triggered by naval competition with Japan following several decades of relative maritime lawlessness.[22] The second phase fell within the Qing period, the late eighteenth and early nineteenth centuries, and was associated with the European presence. Focal points of trade included Canton, where European trade was concentrated, Amoy, Fuzhou, Portuguese Macao, Taiwan, and Spanish Manila, where there was a Chinese community. The predominantly Muslim port of Banten (Bantam), on the coast of Java, was the focal point of Chinese trade in Southeast Asia; in 1682, the Dutch took Banten into their sphere of influence. Japan, a source of much of the silver that reached China, was by this time playing a significant East Asian maritime role despite its relative lack of contact with Muslim networks and its closure to most Europeans.

Muslims, per se, whether Chinese or foreign, had a much lower profile in maritime China than they had in the past. Now most import and export was in the hands of *Chinese* merchants and port officials; some of these men were Muslim, but they had blended into Chinese commercial patterns. Chinese ships seldom sailed further west than the Thai coast. While the Muslim maritime networks no longer seemed to extend directly to China's ports, they still had access to the China trade indirectly in Southeast Asia. A European observer noted in the seventeenth century that some Chinese "turned Javanese," that is, converted to Islam and changed their political and cultural identity.[23] References to Chinese Muslim merchants are few and inconclusive. For example, a Dutch source reported that in 1661 Indian Muslims from the Coromandel coast had sent shiploads of merchandise to Vietnam and Japan, in partnership with Chinese Muslim merchants, with the hope of forging a commercial relationship. The outcome is unclear and, in any case, must have been limited.[24]

Better documentation shifts historical attention to the foreign Muslims concentrated in the northwest, who were sometimes perceived as an economic or political threat by the Ming and Qing.[25] Soon after the Ming came to power, in 1368, they claimed tribute and submission from Timur, the military ruler of the major Islamic regime of Central Asia. Timur, however, clearly did not consider himself to be subordinate. He launched an invasion of China but died, in 1405, before he could acquire any territory.[26] After his state collapsed in about 1450, Islamic polities of Central Asia were far smaller and not often threatening to China. The major issue of contention was control over caravan trade.

Despite the occasional perception of external threat, Ming policy within China was generally tolerant of Muslims, who continued to hold positions of prestige and influence as they had during the Yuan period. A few foreign Muslims became sinicized, even to the extent of becoming Confucian scholar-bureaucrats; most, however, retained a distinct culture and identity and maintained contact with the wider Islamic world through Muslim Central Asia.[27] Foreign Muslims in northwestern China provided essential services: the conduct of trade, such as the export of tea, and the raising of horses and camels needed by the Chinese. For reasons inadequately understood, during the sixteenth and early seventeenth centuries, Muslims revolted against Ming rule several times. The cause may have been rooted in economic depression. Muslims also figured prominently in wider rebellions of the seventeenth century that contributed to the fall of the Ming in 1644. After that, blame for continued economic difficulties was placed on the Qing regime, and Muslims then sided with Ming loyalists. During the Qing era, there was a shift in the transport of tea from the caravan route to the coast, which cut into the trade economy of the northwest.[28] Also, taxation on trade was considered burdensome. As the Qing attempted to expand political control farther into Central Asia in the seventeenth through nineteenth centuries, revolts against them in the region tended to be decidedly Muslim in composition and ideology.[29] Nevertheless, Qing expansion had the effect of including more Muslims within the Chinese empire.

While Muslims still figured prominently in interior China and in overland trade, their role in coastal China diminished. Islamic and Chinese
maritime histories diverged considerably. The acculturation of Chinese
Muslims, the sinicizing of port administrations, and restrictive government policies all contributed to this situation. It was the case, too, that
China was not experiencing economic growth or technological innova-
tion comparable to that of the Song era and, therefore, did not stimulate
Indian Ocean trade, navigation, and shipbuilding as it had in the past.

A Comparative View

For all the imperial powers of Asia, the seventeenth century held difficult
times. In the previous century, there had been a sharp increase in the
population of many parts of Asia, related to an increase in food production made possible by the introduction of crops from the Americas, such
as yams, potatoes, peanuts, and corn, that could grow in poor, previously uncultivated soil. In the seventeenth century, however, population
growth outstripped new food production, a situation that led to inflation
and to taxation that was exorbitant but never adequate to the needs of
the states. There were also drought and disease in many parts of Asia between about 1630 and 1650.[30] These problems led to disaffection among
both peasants and regionally based elites, including provincial military
officers.[31] Also, the Ottomans and the Ming (as well as seventeenth-century Safavids and Mughals, for that matter) had reached their geographic limits of expansion, although they may not have realized it at
the time. Thus, no new tax bases could be conquered and, in fact, some
were lost. To the west, the Ottomans were forced out of Hungary in 1699.
To the east, they found themselves competing with Shah Abbas for territory and for the silk trade. Around the turn of the seventeenth century,
the Ming overextended their military resources and began to experience
stiff competition in mainland Southeast Asia and from the Japanese in
Korea, while the Manchus flexed their muscles in the north.

All of this resulted in political upheaval and breakdown of law and order during the seventeenth century and well into the eighteenth. The Ottoman heartland of Asia Minor saw regional military revolts against Istanbul and the emergence of bandit gangs and later the spread of
Wahhabi influence in Arabian areas claimed by Istanbul. In China, there
were both urban and rural uprisings—including those of Muslims in the
northwest, described previously—as well as banditry, all of which
opened the door to Manchu conquest. The Mughals had to confront
Rajput and Jat uprisings, while the Safavids fell to an Afghani incursion.[32] Imperial responses proved inadequate to internal economic and
political problems. All this happened as the Dutch and English were

making their maritime presence felt throughout Asia. Despite indications of new maritime interests, the distracted imperial regimes provide a somewhat remote backdrop for coastal merchants, to whom we now turn. It is important to consider how these men conducted their transactions, what role Islam played, and how Europeans fit into this world that was still dominated by Muslims.

Asian and Muslim Trade

Muslim maritime merchants were, by and large, involved in the *carrying* trade. They were not usually involved in the larger economic linkage of production with export-import. A notable exception was the Safavid monopoly over the production and export of silk. The usual circumstances of the carrying trade, however, have generated numerous questions in the literature regarding the nature of Asian maritime trade, especially in the three centuries under consideration. One persistent question is whether Asian traders were mostly peddlers.[33] This question involves issues of size and level of organization: maritime peddlers have been defined as merchants of limited means who bought small quantities of goods, leased space on a vessel, and typically accompanied their merchandise. A conclusion that most Asian maritime merchants, including predominant Muslims, fit this definition would have implications for any comparisons made between Asian and Western European trade. Evidence from contemporary European travelers and merchants suggests peddling was pervasive in Asia. Trade was generally not organized into corporate bodies, such as the exceptional Karimis in Egypt or the Hindu guilds of earlier times.

However, between the fifteenth and seventeenth centuries, there is evidence of increasingly sophisticated, larger scale commerce. Various types of partnerships existed and bills of exchange provided a means of credit.[34] Muslim moneylenders, *sarrafs,* who circumvented the restrictions against interest, continued to provide banking services as they had since early Islamic times, while certain Hindu sub-castes did the same for their communities.[35] The administration of commercial and maritime law at each port was overseen by an official who was either chosen by the resident merchants themselves or appointed by a government able to exert that kind of influence.[36] Ship size and cargo capacity were increasing. At least by the sixteenth century, bulk quantities of inexpensive commodities, such as common textiles and grains, required considerable initial investment, usually supplied by a group of wealthy merchants.[37] By the seventeenth century, there are records of private individuals owning large ships.[38] Peddling seems an inappropriate term for such conditions. There clearly were levels of trade that required capital formation.[39] Some would argue that this situation was not true capitalism, depending on how the term is defined; others see it as merchant capitalism, as distinct from financial (banking) capitalism, bureaucratic capitalism of the tax-collecting elite, or the later industrial capitalism associated with Western Europe. If merchant capitalism is defined as capital accumulated from and reinvested in trade,[40] then there were in this era increases in the scale and scope of merchant capitalism in Asia, which enabled Asians to compete at the local and regional levels with European merchant capitalists, even though the structures of their economic systems were not the same.

There was also during this era Muslim political expansion, which tied some areas of production and agrarian taxation to maritime enterprise. For example, in Southeast Asia, notably on Java, several Hindu-Buddhist principalities were conquered by Muslims and exposed to Islamization. We know most about this expansion and Islamization for the sixteenth and seventeenth centuries, as the Europeans were making their presence felt and were recording what they saw.[41] In 1605, the rulers of the port of Makassar, near the southwestern tip of the largest Celebes island, converted to Islam, and they embarked on a sporadic naval campaign over the next thirty-five years referred to as the "Islam wars," during which several nearby ports were forced to embrace Islam.[42] Before 1500, such Muslim military activity can be inferred, as in the case of Majapahit;[43] due to scant documentation, however, it is usually assumed to have been absent. That assumption contributes to a generalization that Islam spread peacefully in Southeast Asia.[44] In fact, political expansion there echoes the aggressive state-building impetus of the earliest era of Islam; it is also consistent with increasing sophistication in the organization and financing of trade.

Another area of debate relates specifically to Islam's role in Asian maritime trade. Islamic jurisprudence prohibited interest and provided favorable customs rates for Muslims. Both stipulations favored networking among Muslim merchants. Both were ideals that were not always and everywhere employed, but there is evidence that they were well known.[45] Networking could be accomplished through an Islamic state or through individuals, but both types are extremely difficult to document. When and where Muslims were in the majority, when and where they were in political power, networks—for the historian trying to trace them—are camouflaged by those very circumstances. In other words, if most merchants in the pool were Muslim, it was not necessarily by design that Muslims dealt extensively with each other, but rather it simply could have been an artifact of probability. The issue is further confused by the fact that various Muslims involved in a transaction might have had different ethnicities and languages, but their Arabic Muslim names appear undifferentiated in the sources. Networks could also be obscured from historians by the wide use of service providers from outside Islam—Hindus, Jews, Armenians—people such as brokers, moneylenders, and insurers. The easiest way to find Muslim networks is to look at the better-documented commercial enterprises established by small coastal states, rather than those of individuals. A Muslim ruler, for example, might have exchanged commercial brokers as well as political agents with another Muslim ruler.[46] He might have acquired control over distant ports and then sent members of his ruling family to oversee trade.[47] These initial efforts were often followed by settlements, enclaves that looked out over the ocean for their cultural and commercial connections. If it is accepted that the expression "Muslim trade" means something more than shorthand for the trade carried on by merchants who happened to be Muslim, then the expression can be used to refer to these cohesive enterprises. It should be emphazised that networks of Muslims were not based on a legal concept and they were not companies or corporations; there was no provision in Islamic law for a corporate person. Rather, they were made up of individuals with interconnected objectives.

Networks show up more clearly for minority groups, such as Jews and Armenians, and for distinct merchant sub-castes in India. Each group was likely to have a high degree of internal homogeneity in terms of enthnicity and language. The designation "trade diaspora" has been applied to such a network in which minority cooperation was sought not only to facilitate trade but also to help preserve the minority group.[48] A well-known individual who provides evidence of such minority networks is Havannes Joughayetsi, a seventeenth-century merchant from the Armenian community on the outskirts of Isfahan, the Safavid capital city. The community had been established earlier by Shah Abbas, through forced relocation from Armenia, in order to serve the commercial interests of the regime. It became the most important center of Armenian networks extending from London and Amsterdam to Canton and Manila.[49] Hovannes traveled extensively, particularly in India. He kept a journal, which is extant for the years 1682 to 1693 and in which he indicates his dependence on distant Armenians for their hospitality and for their ability to serve as translators for his commercial transactions.[50]

Even when they lived in minority enclaves, Muslims did not have the same kind of minority concerns as did Jews and Armenians because Muslims were numerous and Islamic imperial powers ensured that the Muslim community as a whole would thrive. Also, Muslims were not subject to the same caste restrictions as Hindus, although caste-like differentiations survived conversion in India. If, then, minority status and caste restrictions were not motivations, why would Muslims choose networking in the first place? Most simply, networks helped counterbalance the diversity and uncertainty of commercial variables. In the vast Indian Ocean region, weights, measures, coinage, and exchange rates differed from port to port, and prices were not predictable.[51] This situation necessitated distant business contacts and reliable information. Also, since the monsoons delimited arrival and departure times, it was useful to have agents in various ports who could purchase commodities when the prices were low and warehouse them until they could be sold at an attractive profit.

But why *Muslim* networks? The process of networking provided a structure for the apparent preference of many Muslim merchants to deal with coreligionists. As mentioned earlier, a very important element in the common culture was the commercial law provided by Islamic jurisprudence. Commercial law was often observed in the breach, but at least it provided a standard from which to deviate. Beyond that standard, there was a commonality of Islamic culture which overlay distinct and potentially divisive regional variations. The common culture included the Qur'an, communal prayer and other rituals, dietary restrictions against pork and alcohol, regulations about family and social relationships, mosques, and, for many, sufi affiliations. There were often marriage ties between the merchant class and the ulama.[52] Many Muslims had at least a passing knowledge of Arabic or Persian, and even a smattering of common language was advantageous in trade.

As mentioned in Chapter 2, the sufi tradition had generated brotherhoods that often provided room and board for merchants and other travelers. In the maritime world, one such organization was the Kazaruniyya, named for the Iranian hometown, Kazarun, of its eleventh-century founding saint, Abu Ishaq Ibrahim ibn Shahriyar. By the thirteenth century, adherents had spread to ports along the coast of India and in China. Like several other sufi groups, this one sold spiritual insurance: merchants would enter into an agreement whereby they accepted *baraka*, "blessing," meaning here the protective blessing derived from the virtue of the order's dead founder, in exchange for a payment upon the safe completion of a commercial journey. Ibn Battuta remarked on this practice and the presence of the Kazaruniyya at Cambay, Calicut, and Quilon in India and also at Canton in China. Presumably, all their clients were Muslims.[53]

A powerful symbol of the universality of Islam amid plurality was the pilgrimage to Mecca, the *hajj,* required once in the lifetimes of all Muslims physically and financially able to make the journey. The hajj takes place during the last month of the Muslim lunar calendar, and the rituals require several days. People have always come from all over the Islamic world by land and sea. In the period in question, transportation to

Mecca was an annual boon to the maritime industry, as large numbers of paying pilgrims crowded onto merchant ships sailing to Mecca's Red Sea port, Jidda. Many merchants themselves proudly used the title *hajji*, indicating that they had fulfilled the pilgrimage obligation. A merchant community in Southeast Asia had a saying: If one of them had silver, he would buy gold, but if he prospered further, he would go to Mecca.[54] Professional merchants from throughout the Islamic world assembled along with the general throng of pilgrims, and even many of these latter brought with them something to sell in order to help finance their journey. International transactions could be carried out, information could be shared and disseminated. A French source from the early eighteenth century describes the hajj as perhaps the world's greatest trade fair conducted in a short space of time.[55] This commercially significant event was, by definition, exclusive to Muslims.

The components of religious identity mentioned so far had positive effects *within* the Muslim networks. There were some negative effects as well. Two examples, from the many available, of clashes between Hindus and Muslims are given here. The first incident occurred in 1669, when Aurangzeb's Islamization policy reached Surat, the Mughal empire's principal port, in the form of orders to suppress Hinduism. The effects were severe enough to cause Hindu merchants to leave the city in protest, thereby disrupting trade and shutting down many of the commercial services on which the port relied. They returned only after promises of fair treatment were made by government officials.[56] The second example dates from the 1780s, in Sind. In that decade, an intolerant Muslim regime called the Talpurs came to power and began persecuting Hindus. As in the Surat example, this practice only had the effect of seriously disrupting trade for everyone.[57]

European Participation

Another major question that may be asked in this context is how Europeans fit into the well-established trade patterns. This issue is distinct from European dominance over long-distance East-West routes because it involves local and regional trade. There were at least two reasons why European companies or their employees became involved in local and regional Asian trade. One was more or less official: the companies needed to help finance their long-distance trade. The other was unofficial: individual company "servants," as employees were called, needed to supplement their meager salaries.[58]

Before an answer on European participation is hazarded, it should be pointed out that introducing Europeans into the picture greatly enlarges the pool of sources. Books by Western merchants and travelers abounded in an era when the information they could provide was very valuable. Several European countries had trading companies in Asia and each kept records, often in considerable detail and in hand-copied triplicate, many of which have survived in archives. The companies, of course, were interested in their own affairs rather than in those of Asians, but scattered observations and occasional reports on Asian trade are valuable. It is difficult to overestimate the historiographical significance of the increasing amount of documentation, because it skews the story toward Europeans. No longer do a few works, such as the *Suma Oriental* of Tomé Pires, stand out; by the time the British dismantled the East India Company in the mid-nineteenth century, a large building was required to house a set of the company's archives in London. Asians kept current customs registers and shipping lists but often regarded them as ephemeral information not worthy of archives. The Ottomans provide an exception, since their bureaucracy kept land, tax, and legal records. The Ottoman archives are indispensible for Mediterranean history but so far have not proven to be of great help for Asian maritime history beyond the Red Sea and Persian Gulf regions.

The European penchant for record-keeping may have been a dynamic factor in and of itself. Europeans could analyze their data over a long period of time and make adjustments in their business practices accordingly. Long-standing records and decisions based on them lent a corporateness to their enterprise that is not apparent in the Asian case. However, while documentation by Europeans may have had an impact on East-West trade, it did not especially work to their advantage in an Asian setting.

It is not easy to estimate the impact that either the companies or their employees had on local trade. The difficulty is not only the lopsidedness of sources but also the fact that European policies, meant to enhance long-distance trade, had local consequences. An example is the Dutch policy to exclude the English from the long-distance pepper trade from Southeast Asia to Europe.[59] Partly as a result of this closed trade, Bengali merchants accustomed to doing business at Melaka or Java tended to shift to the South Asian Coromandel coast and buy and sell different commodities. This sort of shift had ripple effects that are immediately ascribed to Bengalis but are ultimately attributable to the Dutch.

Europeans had both advantages and vulnerabilities in the Asian markets. It was expected, for example, that Europeans would pay higher prices than anyone else, would buy in larger volume, and would pay cash. In some cases, these expectations provided an incentive to court European merchants by offering prices and rates in their favor. An example is the coffee trade at Mocha, in the Yemen, during the seventeenth and eighteenth centuries. In the early 1770s, Muslims who traded at Mocha paid seven percent import duties and up to eight percent more in various fees; the English were asked to pay only three percent plus modest fees.[60] This preferential treatment angered Muslim merchants in Jidda and Cairo.[61] Another, rather different example is the tin trade at Perak, a Muslim port principality on the west coast of the Malay peninsula. During the seventeenth century, Perak was subordinate to the sultanate of Aceh, on Sumatra; but, by the eighteenth century, it was sufficiently independent to negotiate on its own with the Dutch East India Company. The Dutch wanted tin; Perak wanted a steady income. Perak's rulers realized that the only way to secure Dutch patronage was to make sure the Dutch had a vested interest in the port.[62] They therefore drew up a treaty which gave the Dutch rights to all the tin available at Perak. The resulting Dutch monopoly over tin exports kept most other regional and foreign merchants away, since there was nothing else to buy at Perak except some opium and cloth.[63] Mocha and Perak were both secondary ports, each largely dependent on a single commodity and, for those reasons, ready and willing to entice Europeans, even at the risk of alienating their usual customers.

There were several clear disadvantages experienced by the Europeans. One was their higher overhead expense. Their vessels were bigger than local craft and required larger crews. The demand in local markets—as opposed to the long-distance market for which the ships had been built—meant that cargo space was often underutilized. In contrast, the dhows of the Arabian Sea and Persian Gulf could be managed with small crews, and they carried commodities in efficient volume. Europeans were also disadvantaged in relation to specific local trade practices. One such practice was called in Persian *dastgardan*, roughly, "transfering from hand to hand." It consisted of installment purchases, whereby a merchant with limited funds could pay for and acquire goods piecemeal over a period of weeks or even months. This method took patience on the part of both the seller and buyer and proved to be an unattractive method to Europeans accustomed to the immediate transfer of commodities, even when they were purchased on credit.[64] Another problem for Europeans was that they brought with them few commodities desired in Asia, whereas they themselves had a constant demand for Asian pepper, spices, silk, and tea. This situation helps explain why Europeans paid cash and had difficulty financing long-distance trade. Europeans had to work hard to understand and accommodate Asian tastes. Armenian silk merchants operating from Iran could find little in Europe to bring back: some woolen cloth, metal items such as knives and scissors, watches, Venetian glass.[65] There are examples of the English East India Company trying deliberately to enlarge the Indian market for English-made broadcloth. For example, in 1717, the company suggested that Indian merchants be required to wear English cloth when they approached the company's council at Calcutta to transact business. The council responded to its employers that it would be difficult to interfere with clothing traditions and, furthermore, that Indians used broadcloth for purposes other than clothing, such as for floor coverings.[66] As we will see in Chapter 5, it was not until the nineteenth century, after political domination had been imposed, that the British could legislate the import of British-made cotton into India, thereby hurting the local cotton industry. Sometimes Europeans were not adept at marketing even within Asia: the Dutch company, for example, failed to interest Middle Eastern consumers in Javanese coffee, since they had already developed a taste for the Yemeni variety exported from Mocha.[67] Other areas in which Europeans had difficulty were in money lending and insurance. There were several European-owned agency houses which offered banking services and insurance. They were seldom able to attract Asian customers for the simple reason that such services were already well provided by other Asians.[68]

Before examining, in the next chapter, the competitive impact of European companies, it might be useful to consider the frustrations of an individual company agent named Samuel Manesty who, on his own behalf, often did business in partnership with Asians. Manesty served as the British East India Company's resident at Basra; his term of office was lengthy, extending from the late eighteenth into the early nineteenth century. He was successful enough as a private merchant to be able to buy his own vessels but could never exert the influence he clearly desired. Manesty's job description, as resident, was to facilitate company business at the Ottoman end of the Persian Gulf. However, he tended to reserve his business acumen for his private trade and regarded his official capacity as essentially political. He was periodically reprimanded from London for neglecting the company's trade.[69] While he was the resident, the company was trying to walk a fine line between two mutually hostile polities, namely, the Ottoman province of southern Iraq and the current regime of Iran, which, by the 1790s, was the Qajar dynasty. Manesty did not help matters by getting into squabbles with the Ottoman provincial lieutenant-governor, the *mutasallim*. As the result of one such clash, in 1793, Manesty decided independently to move the residency from Basra to the port of Kuwait.[70] His surprised and embarrassed superiors had to cajole him back to Basra and smooth things over with the Ottomans. Why he was allowed to keep his job for so long appears to be inexplicable.

Manesty's frustrations as a private merchant are amply demonstrated by an incident of piracy. One of Manesty's ships, called the *Pearl*, was often hired out to his own employer, the East India Company. On one such occasion, in the autumn of 1799, the ship carried commodities belonging to various Asian and European interests, including horses owned by Manesty himself. A French pirate seized the *Pearl* and sold the cargo at the Omani port of Muscat. The British regarded the individual Frenchman's behavior as an act of war. In addition, the authorities at Muscat had recently signed a friendship pact with the British, ostensibly to the exclusion of the French, and this appeared to be a violation of that agreement. Because the *Pearl* had been to their port several times in the past, the Muscatis probably recognized it and knew that both its owner and the lessee were British. None of these factors, however, stopped the Muscatis from taking advantage of the bargains offered by the French pirate. The angry British were limited in their reaction by their political concerns. Wanting to maintain the new friendship with Muscat, they chose a low-key response of diplomatic protest. There was little that Manesty, as an individual, could do about his ship or his horses.[71] Enmeshed in its own regional complexities, there was little the company could do either. Manesty's experiences help illustrate both the successes and the limitations of Europeans involved in the local and regional trade during this period.

5 Maritime Competition, Circa 1500–1860

Europeans in Asia

In the late fifteenth and early sixteenth centuries, Europeans learned what Asians already knew: how to use the wind systems of the Indian Ocean. They also learned the wind systems of the Atlantic and Pacific, knowledge which would give them an advantage on a global scale. However, they entered Asian waters before European naval technology greatly exceeded that of Asia and before the Industrial Revolution.[1] By many measures, economic productivity in China and possibly also in India was still ahead of that in Europe.[2] Asia had a relatively large population and possessed urban cultures that were highly complex. The role that Europeans would play in Asia was not at all obvious.

When the Europeans arrived in Asia at the turn of the sixteenth century, there were four powerful land-based Asian regimes: Ming China, Mughal India, Safavid Iran, and the Ottoman Empire, the last three Muslim dominated. The Ottomans extended their political control nearly to Vienna. They—and, by emotional extension, Muslims in general—were perceived as a military and cultural threat to the heart of Europe. Iberians also had the memory of Muslim conquest and of a centuries-long occupation that had only recently been ended, in 1492. This perception of threat colored the views of Europeans who sailed into Asian waters. The land-based strength of Asia and the European fear of Islamic expansion were important elements in the early phase of contact.

By the mid-nineteenth century, for reasons discussed in this chapter, perceptions were very different. The Qing successors to the Ming of China had been compelled to open several of their ports to Western trade, and Europeans were beginning to have economic and cultural impact in some Chinese coastal areas. The Safavids were long gone, replaced eventually by the less effective Qajar regime. The last figurehead Mughal shah lost his East India Company pension in 1858, and minor principalities were unable to resist annexation to British India. The Ottomans were the last cohesive Islamic empire, but they had suffered military and territorial losses already to Russians and Austrians, beginning in 1699 with the Hapsburg recovery of Hungary. By 1850, European military and political power were obvious threats; the existence of a world system, a world economy based in Europe, was, at the time, a more subtle but also a more profound challenge.

The Portuguese

The Europeans in Asia who have drawn the most scholarly attention are the Portuguese, the Dutch, and the English (British after 1701), each of whom formed companies to trade in Asia. It is useful to begin with sketches of each of these powers, then to assess their impact, and finally to consider Muslim responses to their presence. The Portuguese were the first to arrive, and from the sixteenth century into the early seventeenth, they appeared successful. They secured enclaves in ports from Africa to China (Map 5.1): Mozambique, Kilwa, and Mombasa in East Africa; Hurmuz at the entrance to the Persian Gulf; and Cochin, Diu, and Goa in western India, where they also established the port of Bombay. They seized Muslim Melaka in 1511 and acquired from the Ming dynasty permission to have a trade establishment at Macao, near Canton, in 1557.

Vasco de Gama declared that the Portuguese had come to the Indian Ocean seeking not only spices and pepper but Christians as well. Some of these Christians, potential allies, were associated with Prestor John, a supposed twelfth-century monk and ruler in the vague East. The existence of Christian communities in India and Ethiopia fed this legend.[3] The Portuguese were also interested in finding the burial place of St. Thomas, believed to be in southern India, where there were ancient Christian enclaves. In 1518, on the Coromandel coast, a tomb was identified as that of the apostle.[4] Religious solidarity, however, was not the overriding motivation: global Portuguese maritime policy was pragmatic, aimed as competitively against coreligionists of Europe (e.g., Italians) as against Asians. With that in mind, it is easy to see that Muslims were a particular target of negative Portuguese religious zeal not only because Islam was considered a proximate threat and a heresy worthy of refutation but also because Muslim dominance of Indian Ocean trade was obvious, and if the Portuguese wanted to make any headway, they knew it would be necessary to weaken the hold exerted by Muslims. These Portuguese traders earned a mixed but generally negative reputation. There are accounts of brutal acts against and intolerance of Asians. Licentious, unchristian behavior at Melaka drew the sharp criticism of the Basque Jesuit Francis Xavier, criticism that is reminiscent of Ibn Majid's comments about fellow Muslims at the same port years earlier.[5] The Portuguese demand for goods, however, often stimulated new eco-

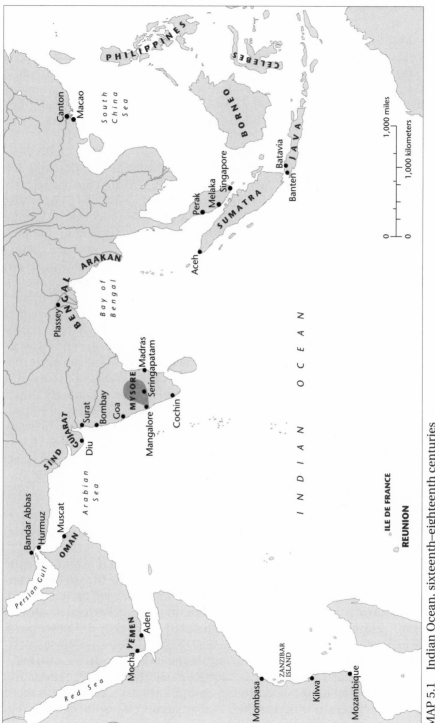

MAP 5.1 Indian Ocean, sixteenth–eighteenth centuries

nomic opportunities for Asians. Some Portuguese blended into the local environment, married or cohabited with Asian women, and produced offspring of mixed culture. A prominent example is Miquel Ferreira, a former ambassador to the Safavids of Iran, who settled on the Coromandel coast—not far from St. Thomas's tomb—with his common-law South Asian wife and their children and maintained his own fleet of vessels.[6]

Trade remained the primary objective. The Casa da India was Portugal's monopolistic trading company based in Lisbon, while Estado da India designated the enterprise in Asia. Private Portuguese merchants participated as well as the crown. Southeast Asian pepper was the most attractive commodity, although profit from its sale in Europe was often disappointing. To bolster the enterprise, the Estado sold protection to Asian and other merchants. This system meant that a trading vessel carrying a pass as proof of payment, known as a *cartaz,* would not be subject to seizure by the Portuguese, while all others were fair game. The underlying idea was simple: threaten violence and then sell protection against it.[7] The system was later emulated to some extent by other European powers and by Asians because it at least seemed like a profitable idea. However, there is evidence that the Portuguese cartaz was often regarded by Asians as a minor tax which did not significantly restrict trade.[8] Also, much of the proceeds stayed in the pockets of Estado officials instead of reaching Lisbon.[9] This problem was a relatively minor organizational flaw. The real difficulty was the impracticality of imposing the pass system over so vast a region, in which it was easy to evade the Portuguese. After the northern European companies arrived, it was even more difficult to impose a national monopoly because of naval competition. Other problems, too, contributed to the failure of the Portuguese enterprise in Asia: inadequate political and financial backing from home and a shortage of manpower.[10]

The Northern Europeans

The other major European powers in the Indian Ocean region were the Dutch and the English, both of whom arrived near the turn of the seventeenth century, at a time when Portugal and Spain were united under a single crown (1580–1640). The presence in Asia of Portuguese armed ships and coastal fortresses made it predictable that the newcomers would arrive prepared to fight as well as to trade.[11] Inter-European maritime hostility was prominent not only in the Indian Ocean but also in regions of Spanish focus, that is, along the shores of the Americas and across the Pacific to Manila in the Philippines. Arguably, the northern Europeans were as brutal as their Iberian predecessors but come across better because they—especially the British—have had considerable influence over the historiography of the period.[12]

Both the Dutch and the English were represented by joint-stock companies embodying mercantilist philosophy. The former were under tighter control by their government than the English and had longer-term investments to start with, but both had monopoly privileges. National monopolies over long-distance trade were intended to close out competition from independent Dutch and English traders, who then had to turn to freebooting and interloping or the purchase of special permits. (Despite these monopoly restrictions, the independent Europeans eventually became influential enough, in the second half of the eighteenth century, to help undermine mercantilism.) The Dutch and English companies were permitted to raise military forces and to make war and peace, powers originally intended to give the companies leverage not against Asians but against the Portuguese. The English assisted the Persian Safavid regime in expelling the Portuguese from Hurmuz in 1622. The Dutch seized Portuguese Melaka in 1641. Asian waters were now open to wider European activity: the Dutch, the English, and the remaining Portuguese were joined by the Danes and the French. Considerable confidence in regional trade opportunities was reflected in the following appraisal by the Dutch governor, Jan Peterszon Coen, in 1619:

> Piece goods from Gujarat we can barter for pepper and gold on the coast of Sumatra; rials and cottons from the coast of [Coromandel] for pepper in Bantam [Banten]; sandal wood, pepper and rials we can barter for Chinese goods and Chinese gold; we can extract silver from Japan with Chinese goods; piece goods from the Coromandel coast in exchange for spices, other goods and gold from China; from Arabia for spices and various other trifles—one thing leads to another.[13]

Asian Trade Revolutions

What impact did the Europeans have on Asian maritime history and on the commerce dominated by Muslims? Answers to this question have been and in some cases still are being disputed, but the various points of view are instructive in themselves. It used to be thought, for example, that the appearance of the Portuguese in Asian waters was a pivotal event, marking the beginning of European dominance. Now it is generally agreed that the Portuguese, while they made a bad impression, had little long-lasting impact beyond limited Catholic conversion, the stimulation of some local markets, and the introduction of a Portuguese patois as a language of trade. The amount of trade they redirected on their own ships to the Cape of Good Hope or to the Red Sea was small in relation to overall Asian exports.[14]

No one disputes that the northern Europeans had a greater impact on Asia than did the Portuguese, but just why that is so is not resolved. It has been argued that the Dutch and English *revolutionized* Asian trade. The scholar whose name is most closely associated with this view is Niels Steensgaard, introduced in the previous chapter. He has argued that a watershed event occurred in the early seventeenth century, when the English and Safavids ousted the Portuguese from the island of Hurmuz. That entrepôt never regained its former status as the nexus of India-Gulf trade; the role shifted first to Bandar Abbas on the Iranian coast and eventually to Muscat in Oman. According to Steensgaard, the ouster represented Portuguese failure in relation to the northern Europeans. The critical factor identified by Steensgaard is structure.[15] The Dutch and English companies were so structured as to minimize price uncertainties in Europe; better business decisions could be made if the price of a long-distance trade item could be anticipated or controlled. More important for the Asian context, these two companies were organized to internalize their protection costs, a concept that needs some explanation. We have seen already that the Portuguese extorted protection money through a pass system; this money, however, did not cover all their *own* protection costs, that is, the overhead expenses of maintaining ships' cannon and coastal fortresses and of otherwise fending off competitors and marauders. The Dutch and English companies, which had better support from home governments in the first place and which had the power to raise their own armies and navies, incorporated their considerable protection costs into the prices they charged for shipping goods. Thus, there was a direct relationship between trade volume and the ability to secure it.

What did these structural advantages allow the northern Europeans to accomplish? According to Steensgaard, they were able to attract a significant portion of *Asian* caravan trade, in silks and spices, to their safe if expensive sea route and then made greater and more efficient use of the Cape than the Portuguese ever had. Steensgaard's focus is on the redirection of Persian silk *from* the caravan route between Iran and Syria *to* company ships at Iranian ports. The upshot was to take trade away from Asian land-based powers and put it into the hands of Europeans who now dominated the seas.

Steensgaard makes a crucial point. The shift in the trade marked the beginning of a significant change in the balance of power between Europe and Asia. Arguably, however, European impact on Asia and its trade did not develop simply from these structural advantages. The overall impact took a long time and manifested itself variously at different times and places. It is, therefore, possible to identify also a *broad* Asian trade revolution.

While Steensgaard used an impressive array of European archives, his theory has elicited further research particularly among scholars able to use Asian language sources. One such scholar is Bruce Masters, who has studied Aleppo, the Syrian end point of the overland Persian silk route. Using Ottoman Turkish and Arabic sources, he argues that Steensgaard's revolution is too abrupt; that, in fact, the revolution can be regarded as a gradual process beginning in the early seventeenth century and extending well into the nineteenth, when Europeans introduced steamships and railways into Asia.[16] This interpretation involves expanding the concept of a trade revolution to include more than the structural innovations of the Dutch and English companies. It also requires taking into account regional variations. Masters sees the revolutionary process in Aleppo extending from about 1620 to 1750; by that end date, not only had the caravan spice trade been redirected to the sea, but the caravan silk trade had ceased. Silk had not been diverted to the sea route; rather, it was simply no longer available in the necessary quantities. Persian silk production had declined, not primarily because of commercial factors, but because of political instability in Iran.[17] After the death of Shah Abbas, the royal monopoly over silk, under less able leadership, began to erode. The Safavid dynasty was defeated by an Afghani tribal prince in 1722, and with the dynasty went what was left of the monopoly over silk manufacture and export. As long as the monopoly had been operative, the silk trade had resisted redirection; only when production fell did the silk caravan trade decline.

To get a handle on a more diffuse trade revolution extending into the nineteenth century, it is helpful to sketch the history of the two major northern European trading companies from about 1650 to 1850. Within the Indian Ocean region, Asians had many advantages: networks, common languages, familiarity with both local demands and commodity sources. Asians also had their own trade practices for dealing under various conditions, such as a slow market or a low supply of specie. Against all this, the East India companies had at first the structural advantages described by Steensgaard and also superior technology in ships, equipment, guns, and even nautical charts. Yet the companies were hardly unqualified success stories.

The Dutch had commercial establishments, called factories, all over the Indian Ocean region, including at Persian Gulf and Indian ports. From the start, however, the Dutch were most interested in Southeast Asia, possibly because it was at a safe distance from Mughal Surat, Safavid Bandar Abbas, and Ottoman Basra. There was a Dutch enclave on Java as early as 1619, at Batavia, that is, Indonesian Jakarta. From this position, the Dutch attempted to control the flow of pepper and spices from Java, Sumatra, and the Maluku islands, in competition with Muslim Aceh. One of the mechanisms of such control was to draw up contracts with Asian producers, agreeing to buy large quantities at reduced prices, an arrangement that guaranteed high volume sales for the producer and allowed the Dutch to resell with a high profit margin, sometimes as high as a thousand percent.[18] Toward the end of the seventeenth century, the Dutch took control of Banten to increase access to the Chinese merchants who regularly sailed there. The Dutch were doing well but were soon to undermine their own success through poor account-keeping methods, corruption, and overspending. Also, private Dutch merchants regularly evaded the company monopoly. In fact, despite the development of coffee farming on Java, the eighteenth century proved to be disastrous financially for the Dutch. They decided to leave their expensively maintained establishments in the western Indian Ocean and the Persian Gulf, where trade was diminishing anyway, in order to consolidate in Southeast Asia. However, by 1799, the company was bankrupt and the Dutch government had to assume its debts and administrative responsibilities.[19]

The geographic focus of the English was India, where the company became territorially involved, first in Bengal. The economic intention was to influence not only maritime export but also production in the interior. Economic and political considerations involved the British also in the hinterlands of Madras and Bombay. These ports, together with Calcutta in Bengal, became seats of presidencies in the East India Company's administration.

In relation to a broad Asian trade revolution, the experience of the British East India Company warrants special attention. One of the advantages of the company, discussed earlier, was the ability to absorb protection overhead by linking it to trade volume. However, the very protection costs which the British had internalized in the seventeenth century began to rise significantly in the eighteenth century to the point where they became a disadvantage. At the turn of the seventeenth century, the company established a small Bombay Marine to protect its interests at Surat; during the course of the eighteenth century, the Marine was enlarged and regularized into a modest but still costly navy, in order to deal with entrenched piracy along the west coast of India. Also, like the Dutch, the British had difficulty maintaining their monopoly against independent nationals who competed with them, causing another drain on profit. Overhead expenses increased as well when the British had to protect their interests in the territories of India for which they had assumed administrative responsibilities. The high cost of the Seven Years War with the French in India, between 1756 and 1763, can be added to the protection side of the ledger as well. A more general cause for higher protection costs was increased maritime instability related to Asian imperial breakdown, already discussed in Chapter 4. The Ottomans, preoccupied with Austrian and Russian advances, had difficulty holding onto their Basran and east Arabian provinces. The Safavids ceased to rule Iran after 1722. The Mughals lost Surat after 1730 and were restricted to the vicinity of inland Delhi by 1750. There appear to be correlations between these reduced imperial circumstances and both a decrease in consumer demand and an increase in naval competition and piracy. Diminished maritime trade between the Middle East and South Asia was at greater risk and therefore was more expensive to protect. The East India Company tried to absorb some of these costs in its shipping fees but then generally *overpriced* itself in the regional markets. In contrast, local competitors could sail their cheaply run dhows in large convoys for protection instead of maintaining a separate navy.[20]

To compensate for all these expenses, the company sought an increased share of Indian Ocean trade. One way for the East India Company to obtain a larger share was to gain control over a significant port with a minimum of any new hinterland involvement. Singapore was acquired by the British in 1819, giving them an edge over the Dutch at Batavia. Another tactic was to reverse Britain's unfavorable balance of trade with China by finding a product to sell to the Chinese that would more than equal the value of British tea purchases. To this end, the British developed an infamous regional opium trade, selling India-grown opium at the Qing port of Canton. When the Chinese tried to stop the trade, which not only shifted the balance of trade against them but also caused serious social problems, they found themselves outgunned by the British navy. A series of hostilities in the 1840s, collectively known as the Opium War, ended in a settlement whereby more ports beside Canton were opened to the British and other Western merchants. There were other opportunities elsewhere. In the western Indian Ocean, Aden came under British control in 1839, providing a commercial vantage point over the Red Sea. In the Persian Gulf, the British extended their influence indirectly through treaty relationships intended to suppress piracy and maritime conflicts. The most well known of these was the General Treaty of Peace of 1820, which generated the designation Trucial Coast for much of the Arab side of the Gulf.[21] This policy directly reduced protection costs.

The continued presence of the French in the Indian Ocean appeared to threaten British plans to increase their influence. Defeat in India in 1763 caused the French to retreat to the margins, for example, to the island of Réunion (Bourbon) and the Île de France (Mauritius), but they continued to trade and seek allies. The British felt obliged to respond. A clear example of this interaction is the Anglo-French competition for influence at Muscat, the Omani port on the Arabian Sea that had recently become the nexus of Middle East–South Asian trade. In the 1770s, Muscati merchant princes of the ruling family, the Al bu Sa'id, had developed a lucrative slave trade in their East African holdings, especially at Zanzibar and Kilwa, where they established administrations. The principal customers were French. The Muscatis also shipped Indian grain to the Île de France and had offered to allow the French to establish a trade factory at Muscat, a privilege never before offered to a European power.[22] In 1799, one year after Napoléon Bonaparte had invaded Egypt, the British intercepted a vague but friendly letter from Bonaparte to the ruler of Oman.[23] The British company's administration at Bombay worried that these Omani connections might give the French a commercial advantage and provide them with a new opportunity for a comeback in the Indian Ocean region. To dissuade the Muscatis from forming an alliance with the French, a Persian agent in the employ of the British company wrote to a Muscat official in 1800:

> Look upon the friendship and esteem of the English ... as the Soul by which Muskat breathes and has its being, and fly the contamination of French fraternity as you would the plague.[24]

A few years earlier, the highest ranking company official in India, the Governor-General in Calcutta, had written to warn against the bad influence Muscat could expect from the revolutionary French:

> [The French,] after putting their King to death, and abolishing religion, are attempting to create disturbances all over the World, and to introduce the same Anarchy and disorder in other kingdoms.[25]

Such advice and comments were difficult for the Muscatis to accept. Rhetoric, however, was not the only tool on which the British could rely; they could and did use commercial leverage. The East India Company threatened to close British Indian ports, including Bombay, to Muscati merchants.[26] Finally, in 1803, came the first indication that the threats were effective. The French sent an envoy to Muscat preliminary to establishing their invited factory, but the Muscati ruler would not allow the envoy to disembark. Word was sent to the ship that perhaps the envoy should return in better times; because the Muscatis had twenty large vessels at British-controlled ports in Bengal and Malabar, they could not risk commercial reprisal by the East India Company for any hospitality extended to the French.[27]

Once the British asserted such leverage successfully, the Al bu Sa'id gave up much of its India-Gulf trade and instead focused on its colonies in East Africa. After about 1830, the ruler shifted his attention to Zanzibar and made it his primary residence. He developed there an economy based on clove plantations run with African slave labor.[28] This economic relocation away from Oman opened up an even larger role for British trade and political influence in the Gulf. There were related shifts in Arabian Sea trade. For example, the Isma'ili Muslim Khoja community of western India branched out to East Africa and coastal Oman.[29] Also, Hindu merchants from Sind and Kutch moved to Muscat, where they supplied new investment for trade. After the Omani ruler shifted his base to Zanzibar, these Hindus virtually took over the declining Omani trade and found new markets, notably United States' buyers for dates.[30] Often Indians in Oman had British citizenship, which provided certain legal protection to their commerce but also attracted Arab Omani hostility.[31] Thus, British efforts to secure Oman from French influence had not only the intended effect but also altered a complex regional pattern.

British India and the Broad Asian Trade Revolution

The ability to anticipate prices in Europe for Asian goods and the internalized protection costs associated with the Dutch and English companies were enough, in the early seventeenth century, for these companies to outflank the Portuguese and attract a noticeable amount of Asian caravan trade to Dutch and English ships. However, during the eighteenth century, structural superiority was not sufficient for the northern European companies to achieve their goals. The Dutch company, we have already seen, had undermined itself by the end of that century. The British company was still viable but strapped by a large increase in protection costs. The British dealt with this problem by acquiring a larger portion of local and regional commerce. They traded opium to China to redress the trade imbalance resulting from their tea purchases. Adding new ports, such as Singapore and Aden, brought more revenues. Diplomatic victories over the French reduced competion in the Arabian Sea and the Persian Gulf. Also, treaty relationships in the Gulf directly helped reduce protection costs. These were steps in the *broader* Asian trade revolution.

All of these steps, however, were still insufficient to keep the East India Company going. In 1813, it lost its monopoly over Asian trade, an indication that the advocates of free trade had won out over the mercantilists. A policy of free trade meant that private British merchants could compete openly with the company in Asian commerce. In 1833, the East India Company was transformed into a management firm for British India and had to sell off its commercial assets, such as warehouses and cottage industries, often to wealthy South Asian entrepreneurs. The company was then funded by the parliament in London to administer British India. The last straw was the Mutiny of 1857–1858, when a large number of sepoys rose against their British officers in northern India. The protracted, expensive suppression of the revolt broke the management company; it was disbanded and replaced with colonial administration under the crown. Over the course of the preceding decades, there had been in British India a corresponding transition from trade determined by commercial factors to a more complex economy supported by military and political clout. For example, the London government was in a position to legislate to the advantage of industrial Britain. Thus, in India, locally produced cotton cloth was taxed more heavily than British-made imports, a situation which encouraged the export of raw Indian cotton to British mills and the sale of British cotton cloth in India. Ironically, this legislation resulted in a near monopoly over a commodity at a time when free trade was officially espoused.[32]

The broader Asian trade revolution, in which the British played a significant role, had now taken its fundamental shape. The final element was the introduction into Asia of European technology, particularly in the areas of transportation and communication. Railways were built, often to connect inland production with coastal exportation; telegraph lines sped economic and political communications; steamships eventually outpaced sailing ships and changed the maritime world by overcoming some of the natural limitations imposed by the monsoon winds.

The steamship in particular came to symbolize the inharmonious intrusion of the "modern" into a "traditional" world. The first steamships to reach Asia in the 1820s were not as fast as the best contemporary sailing vessels; by the 1840s, the steamships had competition from the new sailing clippers designed for speed. It was not until the development of watertight iron hulls and the opening in 1869 of the shorter Suez Canal route that steamships took a decisive lead over timber sailing ships.[33] Steamships, most of them British, competed successfully with the various sailing vessels of the Indian Ocean but did not replace them. Thus, a dual system of trade evolved.[34] The British steamship lines operated regionally from India; routes from there to the Persian Gulf benefited British and Indian merchants to the detriment of Arab and Persian merchants using dhows and operating from Gulf ports.[35]

Muslim Resistance

The complex European role in maritime Asia did not go unresisted. Three examples of resistance illustrate the perceived challenge to the *Muslim* maritime sphere. The first is that of the Mappila campaign against the Portuguese; the second involves the Aceh regime in Sumatra; and the third is the career of Tipu Sultan of Mysore.

The Mappilas

When the Portuguese arrived in Malabar, or Kerala, there were four Hindu principalities in the region, each with a port town: Quilon, Cochin, Calicut, and Cannanore. Indigenous Muslim converts, referred to as *Mappilas*,[36] and visiting foreign Muslims from the Middle East (*pardesis*) dominated Malabar trade, in which pepper was the major export commodity. The Muslim presence can be traced back to the ninth century and was of significant size by the thirteenth century. Separateness from the Hindu environment elicited a sense of Muslim solidarity symbolized by a shared Qur'anic school at Ponnani, a secondary port between Calicut and Cochin. Over the centuries, there had been conflicts with the Hindu governments and population, but these were mitigated by the rulers' dependence on the crucial economic role played by Muslim merchants. This relationship is best illustrated at Calicut, where Muslims exerted considerable political influence with the ruler, the zamorin.[37] The Portuguese posed a threat to these political accommodations as well as to the maritime commerce on which they rested.

The Portuguese were first able to take from the Muslims control over the importation of horses from Arabia, via Hurmuz, to the inland state of Vijayanagar. They were less successful in their attempt to monopolize pepper exports. Competition was a large problem: many pardesi merchants, wishing to avoid the Portuguese, shifted to Gujarati ports, bringing with them Southeast Asian pepper exported from Aceh.[38] A second problem, from the Portuguese point of view, was that the Mappila merchants were able to evade the Portuguese blockade and reach Gujarati ports with Malabar pepper.[39] Even so, the Portuguese presence altered economic and political arrangements: the Hindu rulers of Malabar, seeing the newcomers as welcome competition to the Muslims, entered into trade agreements and military alliances with them, which undermined Muslim political influence.[40] In reaction, Mappilas sought naval assistance from the Mamluks of Egypt and later from the Ottomans; but as it turned out, the Malabari Muslims had to rely on their own naval capabilities to resist Portuguese force. They also attempted to secede politically from Hindu rule, resulting in a Muslim takeover at Cannanore.

Meanwhile, the regional situation was changing. Hindu Vijayanagar fell in 1565 to the rising Muslim states of Golconda and Bijapur, which stretched across central India from Masulipatnam to Goa. Vijayanagar's fall effectively ended the demand for horses and therefore hurt Portuguese interests. There was also a general if temporary decline in hinterland trade with both Gujarat and Malabar. Nevertheless, defeat of a large Hindu state by its Muslim neighbors inspired the Mappilas. They elevated their campaigns against their Hindu overlords and the Portuguese to the status of *jihad,* holy war. Their enemies, in turn, viewed Mappila resistance as piracy against legitimate trade.[41] In the seventeenth century, as the Portuguese Estado weakened, Malabar merchants recovered their livelihood. Interior India saw a revival of some of its former levels of consumption. As in the past, much of the restored commerce was in the hands of Mappilas, particularly the new ruler of Cannanore. Later, when the Dutch tried to monopolize Malabar pepper, they were ultimately no more successful than the Portuguese had been.[42]

Aceh

When the Portuguese arrived in Southeast Asia, Muslim Melaka was the foremost port, with a thriving transshipping economy and a near monopoly on the export of Southeast Asian pepper. Politically, however, Melaka was weak, a situation usually attributed to the greed and corruption of its ruling elite.[43] The Portuguese, with the help of Chinese and Tamil Hindu merchants who were looking for a greater share of trade, forced out Arab and Indian Muslim merchants and proceeded to dominate the port themselves. The trade of Southeast Asia that had been channeled to Melaka quickly resumed earlier, decentralized patterns. The ruling family of Melaka reorganized itself at the port of Johor at the southern tip of the Malay peninsula, near what would later be British Singapore. Although the Portuguese soon recognized the commercial necessity of allowing Muslim Gujaratis to trade at Melaka again, the Portuguese establishment attracted hostility from the Muslim rulers of local, competitive sultanates. These included Johor, understandably enough, Aceh on the northwestern end of Sumatra, and the southern Maluku spice islands. Johor and Aceh competed against each other to replace Melaka in the *Muslim* network. Aceh won that contest and then fiercely resisted further Portuguese aggrandizement. In that effort, Aceh was commercially assisted by an Indian port, Masulipatnam, which rose to prominence in the sixteenth century. Masulipatnam was in the Muslim state of Golconda, in northern Coromandel, and had cultural and commercial ties with Iran.[44] Thus, competition from the Portuguese stimulated a new sub-pattern of trade.[45]

An intriguing by-product of the Portuguese and later the Dutch and British presence was an increase in Islamic orthodoxy. Competition from Europeans at Indian entrepôts and an increase in overall trade volume led island Southeast Asian Muslims to increase their *direct* trade to and from the Yemen and the Red Sea region, which meant contact with Arabians, Egyptians, and even Turkic Ottomans.[46] Among the Arab merchants involved were orthodox ulama, that is, Qur'an and law experts, who set out to purify the Islam of Southeast Asians, which had been adulterated by local customs and beliefs. This orthodox attention was focused on Aceh but it included the Muslim community at Dutch Batavia as well. Also, the larger number of vessels sailing to the Red Sea increased the opportunities for making the pilgrimage to Mecca, giving more Southeast Asian converts the opportunity to encounter cosmopolitan Islam. There is strong evidence that standard Islamic law, the *sha-ri'a*, was more often applied from the last quarter of the sixteenth century through the eighteenth century than anytime earlier.[47]

In the present context, what is important is that contact with Arabia and with the Ottomans gave Aceh a strong sense of Islamic solidarity. This change was demonstrated in 1563, when an Acenese sultan, Ala'din, sent envoys to Istanbul. The envoys relayed to Ottoman officials that several island rulers had promised to embrace Islam if the Ottoman sultan would assist them against the Portuguese. The Ottomans were preoccupied with an insurrection in the Yemen and managed to send only two supply ships.[48] Nevertheless, Aceh's naval force, which included large armed galleys, consistently managed to repulse Portuguese assaults.[49] While the two supply vessels probably did not inspire much conversion, the trend toward Islam was already under way well before the Portuguese had arrived. Islam was the obvious ideology of resistance to the Portuguese and later to the Dutch. In the 1890s, when the Dutch attempted to curb both the slave trade at Aceh and what they considered piracy based there and to bring the port into their sphere of influence, the stiff resistance was couched in Islamic terms.[50]

Tipu Sultan

The third example of Muslim resistance to the Europeans in the maritime sphere concerns Tipu Sultan, who ruled the principality of Mysore in south central India, roughly equivalent to the modern state of Karnataka. He ruled during the last quarter of the eighteenth century, well after Mughal power had declined. Like other Muslim potentates in India, he represented a minority elite ruling over a Hindu majority. Mysore was largely landlocked but did include a corridor to the port of Mangalore, Tipu's outlet to the Arabian Sea. He used maritime trade as a weapon against his enemies, primarily Hindu neighbors and the British, by establishing favored commercial status between Mangalore and other Muslim-dominated ports along the littorals of the Arabian Sea. He also tried to ally with France against the British, whom he recognized as the greatest single threat to his power. The French were ultimately not very helpful. Tipu fought alone and with notable success against British sepoy forces and their Indian allies on several occasions. The British considered Tipu a major threat and finally pulled out all stops to defeat his forces and take his capital city of Seringapatam in 1799. Tipu died in that last assault. Some British and Indian historians tended to vilify Tipu as a Muslim ruler looking out for his own interests while exploiting Hindus through taxation and forced labor. Another view, prompted largely by Indian Muslim scholars but also held by some Hindu Indian nationalists, has portrayed him as India's last good hope to stop the establishment of British hegemony.[51] To this day, he is both a revered and controversial figure in Indian historiography and in popular culture.[52]

It is important in this context to note that Tipu saw Islam as his ideology of resistance, just as the Mappilas and the rulers of Aceh had. His frequent references to Islam can be construed as rhetorical and were ardent if not pious. He wrote, for example, the following to the figurehead Mughal shah in Delhi, in 1785, in anticipation of renewed fighting with the British:

> This stedfast believer, with a view to the support of the firm religion of Mahommed, undertook the chastisement of the Nazarene tribe [i.e., British Christians]; who, unable to maintain the war waged against them, solicited peace in the most abject manner. ... With the divine aid and blessing of God, it is now again (my) steady determination to set about the total extirpation and destruction of the enemies of the faith.[53]

The Slave Trade

Slavery, the coerced service of persons who could be bought and sold, helps to illustrate the varied, even paradoxical, European impact on Asia. On the one hand, Europeans in the Indian Ocean region purchased slave labor for their own use. They also helped enlarge the scope of indigenously owned slavery because they increased the demand for commodities produced with slave labor. On the other hand, in the nineteenth century, the British sought to abolish slavery indirectly by restricting the slave trade, which resulted in a cultural and economic conflict mainly with Muslims.

Slavery and the slave trade in the Indian Ocean region are not well understood, largely because of poor documentation. There are numerous British sources associated with the abolition movement of the nineteenth century. However, there is a question of credibility. Some historians argue that abolitionists inflated the numbers of slaves in their reports in order to heighten indignation and gain support for their cause.[54] Numbers are also a problem because of high mortality rates, especially in transport. There is an accusation made that accounts of slavery in an Islamic context were sanitized in order to present the sharpest possible contrast with the relatively brutal slavery in the Americas. This sort of contrast was useful both to those who wanted to criticize slave-holders in the Americas and also to those who wanted to argue that the Americas gave the legitimate institution of slavery a bad name.[55] Finally, the numbers reported for slavery and for maritime slave trade do not correspond well because many East African slaves were used within Africa.[56] Yet, it was mostly East African slaves who were transported long distances by sea, while South Asian and Southeast Asian slaves were more often used locally.[57] Despite all the difficulties, it is still possible to focus on maritime—that is, East African—slave trade as an area of European impact.

With the arrival of Europeans in Asia in the sixteenth century, there was an increase in the demand for slave labor in construction and agriculture. The Portuguese used slave labor on their holdings (*prazos*) in East Africa.[58] In the eighteenth century, the French as well as local landowners purchased East African slaves for the plantations on the Île de France and Réunion, which grew sugar, coffee, cotton, and indigo.[59] The British bought East African slaves to use in construction projects at their various Asian establishments.[60] After 1833, when an official attempt was made to stop the export of slaves to British possessions in the Americas, it became more difficult to buy from the usual sources in *West* Africa. As a result, there was greater demand for East African slaves.

The European purchase and use of slaves need to be placed in the regional context. Slavery and the slave trade were long-standing features of the Indian Ocean economy. During most of the period under discussion, Ibadi Muslim merchants from Oman were active in East African slave export to the Middle East and India. Slaves were sold regionally for domestic labor—particularly in the Ottoman Empire—and also to work in various types of agriculture: for example, coffee in the Yemen, dates in Oman, cloves on the islands of Zanzibar and Pemba, grain on the mainland of East Africa. Slaves were also used as pearl fishermen in the Gulf, in construction and transportation, and in some industries, such as weaving at Mogadishu.[61] By the late eighteenth century, the Omanis had effectively colonized strategic East African ports in the sense that permanently settled Omani port officials and merchants controlled the export economy.[62] When the British began their efforts to suppress the slave trade, they were necessarily brought into conflict with Muslims.

Literature on the abolition movement has recently emphasized the economic and pragmatic reasons for it: in an industrializing Europe, where machines and low wage labor were characteristic, it became possible to view agricultural slavery in Asia or the Americas as economically inefficient.[63] Abolition had its altruistic justification as well. At least since the fifteenth century, before industrialization, some influential Europeans had viewed slavery as an unnatural state, a sin against God's natural order.[64] Quakers, the Society of Friends, were consistent in their opposition beginning in the mid-eighteenth century.[65] However, slavery advocates could interpret Biblical passages to their own advantage.

Whatever the relative importance of economic and humanitarian factors, abolition also had a cultural dimension. The Muslim response to attempts at abolition was twofold. First, and perhaps foremost, there was a desire to preserve a lucrative slave trade: reselling a slave often resulted in a large profit margin at a time when other types of trade had become less profitable.[66] The same was true of gunrunning, because guns were often exchanged for slaves in barter.[67] The second aspect of the Muslim response to abolition efforts was their resistance to British interference in their cultural values. Islamic law provided guidelines for the humane treatment of slaves and promoted manumission as a potential source of spiritual benefit to the owner.[68] However, because the Qur'an sanctioned the institution of slavery, no human law could abolish it. Also, slaves often converted to Islam, so ending the slave trade would restrict the spread of the faith.[69] Not only had British policies altered older trade patterns but the British insistence on abolition was construed as an effort to interfere with Muslim life. The eventual end to the slave trade contributed to the disruption of a traditional society.[70]

Conclusion

One way to measure European impact on Muslim maritime trade is to look at changes in a major trade route. The Portuguese had taken ports from dominant Muslim networks, notably Hurmuz and Melaka, and they had established enclaves in western India that gave direct competition to the Gujaratis. It has been argued here, however, that this Asian trade was not lost to Asians but merely shifted. Muslim trade at Melaka found its way to the Muslim sultanate of Aceh. The port of Cambay in the Gujarat region declined not because of Portuguese competition but because Cambay's harbor had become clogged with silt. Trade shifted from Cambay to Muslim-dominated Surat, which became the principal port of the Mughals. Much of the merchandise transshipped from Cambay or Surat went on to Aden, the port at the entrance to the Red Sea and not far from the entrance to the Gulf, controlled by local Muslim rulers or sometimes by the Ottomans. The *old* pattern had been described by Tomé Pires for the turn of the sixteenth century: "Cambay chiefly stretches out two arms, with her right arm she reaches toward Aden and with the other towards Malacca, as the most important places to sail."[71] In the *new* pattern, Surat was the pivot and stretched out its arms to Aceh in the east and Aden, among other ports, to the west (Map 5.2).[72] More pepper reached Europe along this route than by the route around

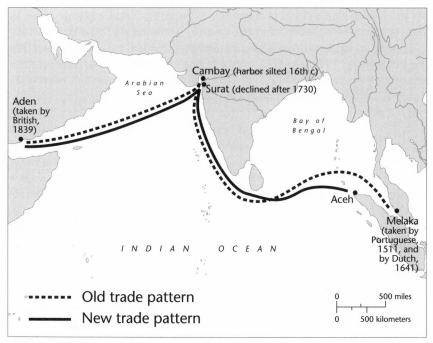

MAP 5.2   Shift in a Muslim-controlled trade pattern, sixteenth–seventeenth centuries

the Cape of Good Hope.[73] The new pattern was weakened by the internal decline in Islamic imperial powers, which reduced stability and regional consumer demand. The Muslim trade pattern was finally broken by the northern Europeans. The Dutch takeover of Banten, beginning in 1682, allowed them to compete with exportation from Aceh. When, for complex reasons, Mughal Surat declined in the 1730s, its replacement on the western coast of India was not another Muslim-dominated port but Bombay, which the British had acquired from the Portuguese in 1661. Finally, in 1829, the British established themselves at Aden. Muslim trade networks did not cease to function, but their visibility and influence diminished. Their decline was imbedded in an ongoing revolution in Asian trade.

This chapter's analysis of the broad Asian trade revolution suggests that *territorial* acquisitions, by the Dutch and particularly by the British, constituted a crucial change, not only by greatly increasing protection costs but by introducing the concomitant excerise of political and military clout. In fact, these imperial and colonial changes made it possible for the Dutch and British to maintain their commercial enterprise, or at least to try to do so, even after the demise of their East India companies.

This point brings us back to the historiographical views introduced at the beginning of the previous chapter. Niels Steensgaard argues that the organization and methods of the northern European companies brought about a commercial revolution in the pre-colonial era, specifically in the early seventeenth century. M. N. Pearson and others aligning with *The Age of Partnership* see an operative Asian maritime economy in which Europeans could participate and to which they adapted before the imperial nineteenth century. Pearson points out that Europe's trade with Asia—and with the Americas—was only a small fraction of Europe's economy before 1750.[74] Considerable evidence can be marshaled for either historiographical view, and neither alone provides a comprehensive explanation.[75] Perhaps it would be useful to put aside, momentarily, the ideological suppositions of those views and try instead to reconcile all the evidence. One way to do so is to recognize two Asian trade revolutions. An earlier, largely structural revolution had some impact on a major Eurasian overland trade pattern, with wide-ranging effects, but did not give Europeans a great advantage in the regional trade of the Indian Ocean. Recognition of a second, broader revolution accommodates the introduction of imperialism, tied to nineteenth-century industrialism, which depended on the use of military and political power and superior technology. Together, they encompass both long-distance East-West trade and equally important regional trade patterns within Asia.

One of the reasons that the historiographical position associated with Steensgaard is criticized is because it seems to suggest that the structural advantages of the Dutch and English companies were the result of an astuteness which Asians could not recognize or match. It is not necessary, however, to infer inherently superior acumen or even the presumption of it. Certainly contemporary Asian practices seemed intelligent to the Europeans. A Florentine visitor to Goa in 1510 commented with enthusiasm:

> We believe ourselves to be the most astute men that one can encounter, and the people here [South Asians] surpass us in everything. And there are Moorish [Muslim] merchants worth 400,000 to 500,000 ducats. And they can do better calculations by memory than we can do with the pen.[76]

Northern Europeans often held similar views. Holden Furber comments:

> Although European entrepreneurs of the seventeenth and eighteenth centuries, thinking and acting in terms of the theories and practices of their own day, believed—at least, most of them—in the superiority of their reli-

gion and civilization, they by no means universally believed in the superiority of their economy.[77]

While there may not have been a general feeling of economic superiority, it would be accurate to say that Europeans, from small countries on a small landmass, had a greater stake in *maritime* power and trade than Asians. Steensgaard points out that in about 1600, the amount of long-distance, seaworthy Asian tonnage in the Indian Ocean was about sixty thousand; in the West, European tonnage was more than half a million.[78] Europeans—notably the British—eventually did break down Muslim hegemony over Asian maritime trade, but the ocean was only of secondary importance to the Islamic world as a whole.

6 Interpretations of the Muslim Era in the Indian Ocean

The introductory chapter posed questions relevant to the intersection of Islamic and Indian Ocean histories. The answers offered here, by way of conclusion, attempt to achieve a synthesis of the material in the foregoing chapters and reflect wide-ranging scholarship.

What Were the Relationships Between Littoral Asia and Land-Based Empires?

In 1573, when the Mughal emperor Akbar was in the seventeenth year of his reign, he visited the newly conquered coast of the Gulf of Cambay, where the ports of Cambay and Surat were located. It was the first time he had ever seen the ocean.[1] The conquest of Gujarat meant that local port revenues could now accrue to Akbar's administration, but it also meant that the goods produced in Gujarat had a larger overland market in the direction of Delhi. There was no immediate change in Mughal maritime policy as a result of either the conquest itself or Akbar's visit; it was left to Akbar's successors to make modest increases in the Mughal fleet. The story conveys an image of a land-based ruler tentatively approaching the maritime world, and the image *seems* to capture the essence of the Asian imperial relationship to the Indian Ocean.

Historians of Asia and historians of the Indian Ocean region rely on each other's work in rather limited ways, a situation that is partly an artifact of land-based imperial priorities, reflected in documentation. Perhaps the best-known example concerns the Ming maritime expeditions. The fact that there *were* such expeditions is significant, but the official records of them are unrevealing, making it difficult to reconstruct motivations and objectives. In the Islamic context, an example with the same sort of ambiguity might be the history of the Karimi merchants, whose rise and demise remain obscure. Also, historians of the Ottoman or Ming empires, for example, rely heavily on the voluminous archives of those regimes. Historians of the Indian Ocean must rely, far more than they would like, on the archives of European trading companies and, especially for earlier periods, on geographical and travel literature written by both Asians and Europeans.

There is a temptation to keep land-based and maritime history separate. Sanjay Subrahmanyam, who has focused much of his research on the Coromandel region during the Portuguese era, urges historians to resist the temptation. At the time Europeans arrived, he argues, some Asian states were developing maritime interests.[2] We have seen this to be true of all the land-based early modern empires. The same was true of the Japanese, whose insular geography forced them beyond their own agrarian economy. Subrahmanyam also offers a more subtle way to integrate land and maritime histories by looking at individuals who crossed the line, that is, men with political or military positions who were also maritime merchants or investors in commodities transported by sea. Some tax farmers in southern India, for example, were merchants who had vested interests in the success of both agricultural production and trade.[3]

However, in large imperial Islamic regimes with military roots, merchants seldom had political positions powerful enough to affect maritime policies.[4] What they *could* do was establish or extend independent principalities in and around port towns. Early examples include ports along the western coast of India. Even the foreign Muslims at Canton in the Tang era, though not politically independent, apparently had considerable control over their own fate, as did Muslim port administrators under the early Yuan. Prominent examples of Muslim merchant principalities after 1400 are Melaka, Aceh, Cannanore, Masulipatnam, Muscat, Kilwa, and Zanzibar. The geography of the oceanic region, including its monsoon systems, did not encourage consolidation of these small polities. Still, merchants achieved far more political success along the littorals of the Indian Ocean than they achieved within the land-based empires.

An obvious connection between maritime trade and land-based empires is the production of commodities for export. Asia's greatest producer of goods was China. The development of Muslim commercial hegemony in the Indian Ocean region corresponds in time to the Tang and Song eras, when the export sector of China's economy grew.[5] Muslim trade networks expanded, particularly in East Africa and Southeast Asia, during the Yuan era, when Muslims enjoyed preferential treatment at Chinese ports. While the decline of Muslim dominance is most readily associated with European competition, especially after 1600, its early manifestations can be traced back to reductions in linkage between Muslim networks and China. Muslim merchants had a lower profile in China after 1430 than they had before. Those who were Ming subjects may have blended into the government-controlled trade system. Foreigners, including Muslims, were less welcome at Ming ports after the end of the Ming expeditions; Muslim Indian Ocean networks, therefore, increasingly obtained Chinese goods in Southeast Asia. While there were periods of industrial growth in China between the sixteenth and nineteenth centuries, such growth was not proportional to the production of exports that had been part of the Song economic revolution of the eleventh and twelfth centuries. Chinese restrictions on foreign contacts and a relative reduction in export production had negative effects on all Asian trade beyond China, including Muslim maritime networks.[6]

How Can We Best Explain the Role Played by West Europeans in the Indian Ocean?

Most discussions of the general European impact on Asia, including the Indian Ocean region, raise controversial *economic* questions. How and when was Asia peripheralized in relation to the European cores of the capitalist world system?[7] Did European imperialism cut short an indigenous Asian development toward industrial capitalism or toward some other system?[8] What encouraged an increase in South Asian production: indigenous population growth or European demand?[9] Some historians posit that there was an Asian vulnerability to European methods of production and trade, a vulnerability attributed to despotic tendencies, that is, overly centralized control over resources and revenues by Asian imperial governments.[10] Definitive answers to all these questions have not yet been found, partly because they require theoretical frameworks flexible enough to encompass the complex variables existing from place to place and time to time. While Muslims figure incidentally in the contexts for these conceptual analyses, Islam, per se, seems to make little difference in the debates, except insofar as Islam is considered to be inconsistent with "oriental despotism" or consistent with (merchant) capitalism. In the present context, with its focus on Muslims, it seems best to make a fresh start in answering the question about European impact.

In some functional—though not structural—ways, the much older Muslim commercial networks resembled the national or company monopolies of the Europeans. Both used methods of credit to facilitate larger volumes of trade. Both tried to establish optimal commercial conditions. For example, the northern European companies often struck deals to secure supplies of commodities at relatively low cost, such as the arrangement made with the Dutch (see Chapter 5) for tin at Perak. Muslim networks attempted to maximize revenues by instructing distant brokers to buy up commodities at a favorable price for resale later when the value rose. While prices could fluctuate freely in Muslim ports, customs rates could be—and often were—manipulated. Also, companies were built around monopolistic charters, while the Muslim networks developed around potentially exclusionary laws and practices, resulting in a competitive edge. If the functions of the networks and companies were similar, why did Muslims lose so much of their maritime position to the northern Europeans? The answer that Europeans had superior naval force and that northern European companies had more effective commercial structures is true but is also perhaps too immediate to be fully accurate.

European impact needs to be set against the long era of Muslim dominance that preceded it and must take into account Asian continental history, first in relation to China and then in relation to Islamic empires. As has been noted in Chapter 4 and in the previous section of this chapter, the development of Muslim dominance over Indian Ocean trade corresponded in time with major changes in China's economy, involving both an increase in demand for foreign goods and an increase in export production. By the ninth century, Muslim merchants established themselves in Indian and Chinese ports as well as those of the Middle East and edged out their Hindu Indian predecessors in the carrying trade from China. When the Chinese economy turned more inward, and when foreigners were less welcome in China after the 1430s, such opportunities dwindled. Also, China lost its global lead in technology, including the naval technology from which merchants had benefited. With regard to Islamic empires, Muslim maritime success coincided with the economic growth and cultural stability of imperial Islam over a large landmass, making possible fairly high consumer demand from the eighth through the seventeenth centuries. When the last major Islamic empires—those of the Ottomans, Safavids, and Mughals—began to weaken, there was a predictable negative effect on their economies that reached the maritime sphere. Commercial momentum carried Muslim maritime networks into the eighteenth century; the networks were successful in shifting their trade patterns to avoid European interference. However, diminished opportunities for growth in the carrying trade, diminished consumer demand within the Muslim-dominated landmass, and the structural and naval strengths of Europeans all combined to undermine Muslim hegemony in the Indian Ocean region. After about 1800, the networks seemed unable or unwilling to reinvent themselves in order to compete with the Dutch and the British in particular.

From the point of view of the Muslim role in maritime history, European impact can be seen *schematically* in the eventual alteration of a major trade pattern connecting western India to both the Middle East and Southeast Asia. The Portuguese introduced the idea of national claims to trade but failed to make much of a dent in the flow of Asian commodities, either long-distance or regional. When they competed for a portion of the major trade pattern by taking Melaka, Muslim trade shifted to Aceh. When the Dutch and English intervened, disruption was more profound. Although at a disadvantage in local and regional trade, the northern Europeans attracted some long-distance caravan trade to the sea route and reorganized protection financing. Later, they opted for territorial acquisition and political involvement, which gave them a degree of control over production, particularly in India. They also availed themselves of technological changes, with far-reaching results. Such European impact has been framed in this book by the two trade revolutions: the early seventeenth-century structural changes introduced by the northern European companies (Steensgaard) and the broader, more diffuse revolution built on territorial and political power in the nineteenth century (e.g., Pearson), even though the trading companies had outlived their usefulness.

A polemical element often enters into discussions of European impact and ties in with some of the historiographical points raised earlier. Subrahmanyam has caught the essence of two extreme positions, and his words are borrowed here to illustrate predispositions:

> An earlier generation of historians, functioning within the paradigm of 'European expansion', tended to take literally the judgements of those who wrote from within the European factory, ship, or trading post. Historians like [K. M.] Panikkar and O. K. Nambiar attempted for their part to rewrite history by turning these judgements over on their heads, producing the image of an age dominated by the unreasoning cruelty of expanding Europeans.[11]

Implicit in the first extreme is an assumption of European activity in relation to Asian passivity. Implicit in the second extreme is a moral judgment against brutal Europeans in relation to peaceful Asians. To counter both these simplistic and dehumanizing interpretive tendencies, it would make sense to compare aggrandizing land-based Asians with aggrandizing maritime Europeans in Asia, that is, to compare the degrees of initiative and levels of violence of the two groups on the bases of their respective political and economic priorities. The astute Mamluk Sultan Baybars wrote to the European king of Cyprus in the 1270s, "Your horses are ships, while our ships are horses."[12] In 1600, more than three centuries later, Asian shipping was perhaps one tenth the size of European shipping, indicating that priorities had not fundamentally changed.[13]

What Difference Did It Make to Be a *Muslim* Merchant?

A scholar of Southeast Asian history has argued that conflicts and competition among Muslim ports indicate that the concept of Muslim solidarity in commerce is a myth. He uses as an example sixteenth-century competitive hostility among Muslim ports, such as Aceh and Johor.[14] What may be overlooked in this line of argument is that the winner was always Muslim and that even the losers continued to be part of a network. When Aceh won regional Muslim supremacy after the Portuguese conquest of Melaka in 1511, an individual merchant could stay in a secondary port such as Johor or move to Aceh.

Muslims *did* establish fluctuating, often interlinking networks—not a single network—over the Indian Ocean region. The high point of this phenomenon came during the late thirteenth and early fourteenth centuries, when Muslim maritime networks, together with their overland counterparts, were important, perhaps critical, to the success of a possible world system connecting Europe and Asia.[15] The maritime networks comprised not only trade routes but also standing business relationships usually based on extended families and/or state structure.[16] The networks generated a commercial hegemony for a long period of time. There was often a clearly dominant regional port serving more than one network. For example, Melaka, then Aceh, drew on local networks as well as those operating in either the Bay of Bengal or the South China Sea. Cambay and then Surat were major links for networks in both the eastern and western Indian Ocean. Siraf, Hurmuz, then Bandar Abbas, and finally Muscat channeled trade networks to and from the Persian Gulf. How restrictive or exclusive Muslim control could have been is indicated by the willingness of some non-Muslims to take advantage of the European presence in hopes of (re)gaining more trade for themselves: Chinese and South Asian Tamil merchants helped the Portuguese take Melaka in 1511; later in that same century, Hindu rulers in Malabar aligned with the Portuguese in a largely unsuccessful attempt to weaken the Muslim position there.[17]

It is useful to ask what role Islam—separate, for the most part, from imperial power—played in the centuries of maritime strength. On what did Muslim maritime supremacy rest? There is no single component of Islam that would provide an easy answer, since the religion was hardly monolithic, encompassing as it did so many regional variations and changes over time. The Isma'ili Fatimids of Egypt, who built up an effective commercial network within a much larger Islamic context, offer compelling examples of doctrinal differences distinguishing them from followers of either Twelver Shi'ism or Sunnism. While the Isma'ilis believed that they represented true Islam, many adherents of orthodoxy were reluctant to consider them brothers in faith.[18] This degree of divergence cautions against overreliance on doctrine or universality to explain Islam's maritime role. Islam provided a framework; it was a portable, legalistic faith, attractive to and suitable for merchants. Yet, there was a wide variety of Muslims who actually exercised commercial dominance.

Sectarian differences deserve further scrutiny. In the imperial situation, sectarian differences often reflected political and territorial competition between land-based regimes, such as the Isma'ili Fatimids and Sunni Saljuqs or the Sunni Ottomans and Shi'i Safavids. This sort of association was less pronounced in the maritime situation. It is true, for example, that the South Asian port of Masulipatnam had Shi'i commitments, due to its historical links with Iran. It is also true that Isma'ilis, Sunnis, and Shi'is tended to network within their respective communities, by choice or circumstance. Commercial competition could degenerate into hostilities, and there were many instances of rhetorical recriminations among the branches and sects of Islam, that is, mutual accusations of un-Islamic doctrines or behavior.[19] Yet, the examples of littoral Islamic subdivisions presented in the foregoing chapters suggest no entrenched political barriers to commerce on a sectarian basis, barriers that might have been damaging to small-scale economies based primarily on the carrying trade.

Muslim maritime supremacy rested partly on certain widely held Islamic values. The impetus to proselytize and to build Islamic states—including small merchant principalities—fit well with economic impulses. The directions in which early Islam expanded correspond well with economic and specifically commercial opportunities. This observation is consistent with both the Middle East's long-established role as a geographic nexus between Europe and the rest of Asia and its dependence on trade as a supplement to agriculture in arid or semi-arid circumstances. Islamic values reflected this legacy, placing honest merchants beside martyrs in the faith. Commerce and even specifically maritime trade enjoyed prestige in the Qur'an and hadith literature. While the military regimes of the middle period may have restricted political access, merchants still enjoyed high status and a significant economic role; they could seek their political fortunes outside imperial structures.

To these general values can be added more specific Islamic cultural elements. Rituals (everything from the avoidance of pork to the hajj), social regulations such as those governing marriage and inheritance, and architectural expressions epitomized by the mosque all drew longtime and convert Muslims together, despite their disparate backgrounds. The law called upon Muslims to avoid imposing interest and to favor coreligionists. The ideal requirement to seek slaves from beyond the Muslim and dhimmi community contributed to the colonization of East Africa. Arabic, the language of the Qu'ran, had some degree of impact everywhere Muslims settled.

Coastal Muslim merchants may have been more self-conscious of their religious identity than their inland counterparts for two reasons. One was abrupt maritime regionalism (as opposed to more gradual cultural transitions on land). For example, a merchant from Mecca might have been culturally shocked by the animism of East Africa or island Southeast Asia and therefore more likely to emphasize his Muslim identity. Evidence supporting this contention can be found in the efforts of Hijazi ulama-merchants to bring orthodoxy to Aceh and Batavia.[20] The second reason, in many cases, was minority status, which often translated into geographically isolated Muslim enclaves, such as those along the coasts of India. Sometimes minority status was more or less permanent, as in Malabar; other times enclaves served as bases for extensive Islamization, as in Sumatra and Zanzibar.

Finally, Islamic commercial law provided a basis for exclusivity, most evident in relation to Hindus in India and Confucians in China. The success of Muslims attracted—even sometimes economically necessitated—conversion. Thus, success encouraged the further spread of a unifying, though not uniform, culture. Exclusivity reinforced religious identity, which in turn was institutionalized in Islamic merchant states. Comparable in important ways to national identity among the Portuguese, Dutch, or British, Islam provided an ideological basis for resistance to economic and political competition.

Notes

Chapter 1

1. Ashin Das Gupta, "India and the Indian Ocean in the Eighteenth Century," in Ashin Das Gupta and M. N. Pearson, eds., *India and the Indian Ocean 1500–1800* (Calcutta: Oxford University Press, 1987), pp. 132–133.

2. M. N. Pearson, "Merchants and States," in James D. Tracy, ed., *The Political Economy of Merchant Empires* (Cambridge: Cambridge University Press, 1991), p. 69.

3. K. N. Chaudhuri, *Trade and Civilisation in the Indian Ocean: An Economic History from the Rise of Islam to 1750* (Cambridge: Cambridge University Press, 1985), e.g., p. 3. Cf. Niels Steensgaard, "The Indian Ocean Network and the Emerging World-Economy, c. 1500–1750," in Satish Chandra, ed., *The Indian Ocean: Explorations in History, Commerce and Politics* (New Delhi: Sage Publications, 1987), p. 127.

4. H. Neville Chittick and Robert I. Rotberg, eds., *East Africa and the Orient: Cultural Syntheses in Pre-Colonial Times* (New York: Africana Publishing Co., 1975), p. 2.

5. Chaudhuri, *Trade and Civilisation*, ch. 5 and maps on pp. 104 and 115. Janet Abu-Lughod, *Before European Hegemony: The World System A.D. 1250–1350* (New York: Oxford University Press, 1989), e.g., pp. 32–38; she includes both maritime and overland loops or circuits.

6. See, for example, Huri̇ Islamoğlu-İnan, "Introduction," in Huri̇ Islamoğlu-İnan, ed., *The Ottoman Empire and the World-Economy* (Cambridge: Cambridge University Press, 1987), p. 3.

7. For a brief discussion of this, see Frederick Mathewson Denny, *An Introduction to Islam,* 2nd edn. (New York: Macmillan Publishing Company, 1994), pp. 195–196.

8. Matthew 22:15–22; Mark 12:13–17; Luke 20:19–26.

9. E.g., Maxime Rodinson, *Islam and Capitalism,* trans. by Brian Pearce (Austin: University of Texas Press, 1978), p. 110.

10. See, for example, Fazlur Rahman, *Islam,* 2nd edn. (Chicago: University of Chicago Press, 1979), chs. 4 and 14. Also, Abdulaziz Abdulhussein Sachedina, *The Just Ruler (al-sultan al-'adil) in Shi'ite Islam* (New York: Oxford University Press, 1988).

11. Stanley Wolpert, *A New History of India,* 4th edn. (New York: Oxford University Press, 1993), pp. 207–208.

12. For the Mediterranean: Henri Pirenne, *Mohammed and Charlemagne,* trans. by B. Miall (New York: W. W. Norton, 1939); Alfred F. Havinghurst, ed., *The Pirenne Thesis: Analysis, Criticism, and Revision* (Boston: D.C. Heath and Com-

pany, 1958). On trade by land and sea: Maurice Lombard, *The Golden Age of Islam*, trans. by Joan Spencer (Amsterdam: North Holland Publishing Co., 1975). For specifically Asian maritime history, see K. N. Chaudhuri, *Asia Before Europe: Economy and Civilisation of the Indian Ocean from the Rise of Islam to 1750* (Cambridge: Cambridge University Press, 1990). In this book, Chaudhuri sees an Indian Ocean life cycle corresponding closely to the rise and decline of Islamic dominance, but his emphasis is on the life cycle rather than on Islam.

13. Chittick and Rotberg, eds., *East Africa and the Orient*.

14. An example of an economic approach: Dietmar Rothermund, *Asian Trade and European Expansion in the Age of Mercantilism* (New Delhi: Manohar, 1981). For port cities as a focus, see Frank Broeze, ed., *Brides of the Sea: Port Cities of Asia from the 16th–20th Centuries* (Honolulu: University of Hawaii Press, 1989). For European trading companies, two very different but classic examples are: K. M. Panikkar, *Asia and Western Dominance: A Survey of the Vasco Da Gama Epoch of Asian History, 1498–1945*, 2nd edn. (London: George Allen & Unwin Ltd., 1959); and Holden Furber, *Rival Empires of Trade in the Orient, 1600–1800* (Minneapolis: University of Minnesota Press, 1976).

15. Fernand Braudel, *The Mediterranean and the Mediterranean World in the Age of Philip II*, trans. by Sian Reynolds, 2 vols. (New York: Harper and Row, 1972–1973). A self-conscious effort to view the Indian Ocean as a maritime space is Chaudhuri, *Trade and Civilisation*. An older, far less theoretical history is Auguste Toussaint, *History of the Indian Ocean*, trans. by June Guicharnaud (Chicago: University of Chicago Press, 1966).

Chapter 2

1. William Montgomery Watt, *Muhammad at Mecca* (Oxford: Clarendon Press, 1953).

2. Patricia Crone, *Meccan Trade and the Rise of Islam* (Princeton: Princeton University Press, 1987).

3. Ibid., pp. 46–50; 246.

4. Ibid., p. 241.

5. In contrast, see ibid., p. 243. Crone argues that expanding the state through conquest does not necessarily indicate interest in or ability to control sophisticated commerce in the conquered areas. Conquest was well within the Arabian tribal repertoire for survival and acquisition of booty; sophisticated commerce, she says, was not. While the imperial powers might have been attracted by commercial possibilities in Arabia, Crone's argument is that sophisticated trade had to be learned by the Arabian Muslims and therefore cannot be used to explain their initial expansion against those imperial powers. Crone diverges in many other significant ways, not mentioned here, from the standard analyses of early Islamic history.

6. Muhammad Shaban, *Islamic History: A New Interpretation*, vol. 1, A.D. 600–750 (A.H. 132) (Cambridge: Cambridge University Press, 1971), ch. 1.

7. E.g., Fred McGraw Donner, *The Early Islamic Conquests* (Princeton: Princeton University Press, 1981), pp. 270–271.

8. Crone, *Meccan Trade*, pp. 133–138 and 243.

9. For an emphasis on the role of merchants in the rise and development of Islam, see Mahmood Ibrahim, *Merchant Capital and Islam* (Austin: University of Texas Press, 1990).

10. The Qur'an, 12:2, 13:37, 41:44, 42:7, 16:103.

11. G. Strenziok, "Azd," *The Encyclopedia of Islam,* 2nd edn. (Leiden: E. J. Brill, 1960–); P. Risso, *Oman and Muscat: An Early Modern History* (London: Croom Helm and New York: St. Martin's Press, 1986), pp. 118–119. The slaves came from the interior and, since Islamic law forbade the enslavement of Muslims, it would have been counter-productive to convert the interior. This disincentive, however, did not apply to the coastal region where the slave markets were located.

12. Derryl MacLean, *Religion and Society in Arab Sind* (Leiden: E. J. Brill, 1989), e.g., pp. 154 ff. From the ninth century, there was some Hindu conversion as well.

13. R. Brunschvig, "'Abd," *The Encyclopedia of Islam,* 2nd edn. (Leiden: E. J. Brill, 1960–).

14. Ralph Austen has tentatively estimated the number of African slaves exported to the Islamic world at about eight million (personal correspondence). This is a lower estimate from figures which appeared in his *African Economic History* (London: James Currey and Portsmouth, NH: Heinemann, 1987), p. 275, table A2. See also his article, "The 19th Century Islamic Slave Trade from East Africa (Swahili and Red Sea Coasts): A Tentative Census," in William Gervase Clarence-Smith, ed., *The Economics of the Indian Ocean Slave Trade in the Nineteenth Century* (London: Frank Cass, 1989).

15. On military slaves see: Patricia Crone, *Slaves on Horses: The Evolution of the Islamic Polity* (Cambridge: Cambridge University Press, 1980); Daniel Pipes, *Slave Soldiers and Islam* (New Haven: Yale University Press, 1981). On slave soldiers thirteenth through seventeenth centuries, see: David Ayalon, *The Mamluk Military Society* (London, 1979); I. Metin Kunt, *The Sultan's Servants: The Transformation of Ottoman Provincial Government, 1550–1650* (New York: Columbia University Press, 1983). For an overview, see Bernard Lewis, *Race and Slavery in the Middle East: An Historical Inquiry* (Oxford: Oxford University Press, 1992). For the late Ottoman context: Ehud R. Toledano, *The Ottoman Slave Trade and Its Suppression: 1840–1890* (Princeton: Princeton University Press, 1982).

16. David Brion Davis, *Slavery and Human Progress* (New York: Oxford University Press, 1984), e.g., ch. 3.

17. This Shi'i use of the word imam should not be confused with its more generic use to designate the prayer leader of a mosque.

18. The eponyms are: Malik ibn Anas of Medina, Abu Hanifa of Kufa, Ahmad ibn Hanbal of Baghdad, Muhammad al-Shafi'i of Medina and Cairo.

19. On the functioning of schools of law, see, for example, George Makdisi, "The Sunni Revival," in D. S. Richards, ed., *Islamic Civilisation, 950–1150* (Oxford: Bruno Cassirer Ltd., 1973).

20. Other examples are 17:66 and 45:12. Sailing the sea for profit is not always interpreted literally as maritime trade but sometimes as a metaphor for spiritual growth.

21. Other examples are 83:1–4 and 2:282–283. These verses can be understood to refer not only to the obvious market transaction but also to general human behavior.

22. Claude Cahen et al., "Hisba," *The Encyclopedia of Islam*, 2nd edn. (Leiden: E. J. Brill, 1960–).

23. W. Heffening, "Sarf," *First Encyclopedia of Islam, 1913–1936* (Leiden: E. J. Brill, 1987). Also, Maxime Rodinson, *Islam and Capitalism*, trans. by Brian Pearce (Austin: University of Texas Press, 1978), pp. 35–37.

24. Muhammad Ali, *A Manual of Hadith* (Brooklyn, NY: Olive Branch Press, 1988), p. 294. For other examples, see M. N. Pearson, "Merchants and States," in James D. Tracy, ed., *The Political Economy of Merchant Empires* (Cambridge: Cambridge University Press, 1991), p. 62.

25. S. D. Goitein, "The Rise of the Near-Eastern Bourgeoisie in Early Islamic Times," *Cahiers d'Histoire Mondiale*, vol. 3 (1957), pp. 584, 586, 594–595. Cf. Ibrahim, *Merchant Capital and Islam*, p. 182: "the Umayyad dynasty guaranteed the hegemony of the Arab merchants and their capital just as the Banu Umayya did in Mecca. ... The position of the merchants, therefore, changed significantly not only in that they came to control an empire, but in that they also came to control its resources."

26. For example, see R. B. Serjeant, "Maritime Customary Law off the Arabian Coasts," in Michel Mollat ed., *Sociétés et compagnies de commerce en Orient et dans l'Océan Indien* (Paris: SEVPEN, 1970).

27. On partnerships, *commenda*, and types of credit, see Abraham Udovitch, *Partnership and Profit in Medieval Islam* (Princeton: Princeton University Press, 1970), esp. ch. 6, for possible Arab origins of commenda and Arabic terminology.

28. A much-quoted source for this type of law is Abu Yusuf, a legal expert who studied with the famous jurist Abu Hanifa (for whom the Hanafi school of law is named); Abu Yusuf died in Baghdad in 798. For a translation and commentary on Abu Yusuf's book on Islamic taxes, see A. Ben Shemesh, *Taxation in Islam*, vol. 3, *Abu Yusuf's 'Kitab al-Kharaj'* (Leiden: E. J. Brill, 1969). The reference here is to p. 140. A jurist of the early tenth century who follows Abu Yusuf closely but not exactly is Qudama b. Ja'far: see ibid., vol. 2, pp. 56–57.

29. Andrew S. Ehrenkreutz, "Bahriyya," *The Encyclopedia of Islam*, 2nd edn., Supplement (Leiden: E. J. Brill, 1980).

30. M. Canard, "Fatimids," *The Encyclopedia of Islam*, 2nd edn. (Leiden: E. J. Brill, 1960–).

31. Bernard Lewis, "The Fatimids and the Route to India in the Xth and XIth Century," *Revue de la Faculté des Sciences Économiques de l'Université d'Istanbul*, vol. 11 (1949–50).

32. On Mahmud of Ghazna, see C. E. Bosworth, *The Ghaznavids* (Edinburgh: Edinburgh University Press, 1963). Bosworth gives booty figures from Muslim sources, which he considers to be exaggerated. From Somnath, for example, Mahmud was said to have taken "over twenty million dinars' worth of spoil" (p. 78). Mahmud's harsh introduction of Islam into northern India can be mitigated by reference to two written accounts of India by roughly contemporary Muslims. One was that of a tenth-century geographer/traveler, al-Mas'udi, who believed that philosophy and science had Indian origins. See Tarif Khalidi, *Islamic Historiography: The Histories of Mas'udi* (Albany: State University of New York Press, 1975), pp. 103–106. The second is a somewhat sympathetic description of Hindus

by an eleventh-century scholar, al-Biruni. An English abridgement of his history of India is: *Alberuni's India,* trans. by Edward C. Sachau, ed. by Ainslie T. Embree (New York: W. W. Norton and Company, 1971).

33. Bosworth, *The Ghaznavids,* pp. 52–53.

34. He sees this coincidence as the beginning of an Asian life-cycle that ends with the onset of British territorial control in India. K. N. Chaudhuri, *Asia Before Europe: Economy and Civilisation of the Indian Ocean from the Rise of Islam to 1750* (Cambridge: Cambridge University Press, 1990), p. 98; also his *Trade and Civilisation in the Indian Ocean: An Economic History from the Rise of Islam to 1750* (Cambridge: Cambridge University Press, 1985), p. 34.

35. G. F. Hudson, "The Medieval Trade of China," in D. S. Richards, ed., *Islam and the Trade of Asia* (Oxford: Bruno Cassirer, 1970), p. 161. On place-of-origin for vessels, see Jung-pang Lo, "Chinese Shipping and East-West Trade from the Tenth to the Fourteenth Century," in Michel Mollat, ed., *Sociétés et compagnies de commerce en Orient et dans l'Océan Indien* (Paris: SEVPEN, 1970), pp. 174–176; also Edward Schafer, *The Golden Peaches of Samarkand* (Berkeley: University of California Press, 1963), pp. 12–13.

36. Schafer, *Golden Peaches,* p. 21.

37. For a compilation of several Arabic references, see Jean Sauvaget, ed. and trans., *Ahbar as-Sin wa l-Hind [Akhbar al-Sin wa al-Hind]: Relation de la Chine et de l'Inde* (Paris, 1948), Sauvaget's introduction, pp. xxxviii–xxxix.

38. Schafer, *Golden Peaches,* p. 24.

39. Ibid., pp. 28–32. Ceramics and porcelains were increasingly important among Chinese exports because silk had been available in Syria since the sixth century and in Persia soon after. Being lightweight, silk was efficiently carried overland; heavier ceramics and porcelains were better carried by sea. Hudson, "The Medieval Trade of China," in Richards, ed., *Islam and the Trade of Asia,* p. 160. See also Shiba Yoshinobu, "Song Foreign Trade: Its Scope and Organization," in Morris Rossabi, ed., *China Among Equals* (Berkeley: University of California Press, 1983), p. 94.

40. Peter B. Golden, "The Karakhanids and Early Islam," in Denis Sinor, ed., *The Cambridge History of Early Inner Asia* (Cambridge: Cambridge University Press, 1990), p. 344. The Muslims reportedly learned how to make paper from Chinese captives taken in this battle.

41. George Hourani, *Arab Seafaring in the Indian Ocean in Ancient and Medieval Times* (Princeton: Princeton University Press, 1951), p. 63. Schafer, *Golden Peaches,* pp. 9 and 16. It has been suggested that these Muslims at Canton were a mercenary force but Schafer believes they were merchants under the leadership of a Chinese pirate, Feng Jo-fang, who was hostile to the government (pp. 282–283, note 77). The Chinese sources, up to 758, refer to Arabs as Dashi (Ta-shih in Wade-Giles) and to Persians as Bosi (Po-sse); after the mid-eighth century, Dashi increasingly became a generic term for Muslims, possibly because non-Arab converts to Islam, including Persians, had taken Arabic names. See Hudson, "The Medieval Trade of China," in Richards, ed., *Islam and the Trade of Asia,* p. 162; also, Hourani, *Arab Seafaring,* pp. 62–63 and 65.

42. Schafer, *Golden Peaches,* pp. 10 and 16; Hourani, *Arab Seafaring,* p. 77.

43. Lo, "Chinese Shipping," in Mollat, ed., *Sociétés and compagnies*, p. 169.

44. Pierre-Yves Manguin, "The Vanishing *Jong:* Insular Southeast Asian Fleets in Trade and War (Fifteenth to Seventeenth Centuries)," in Anthony Reid, ed., *Southeast Asia in the Early Modern Era: Trade, Power and Belief* (Ithaca, NY: Cornell University Press, 1993), p. 204.

45. Jung-pang Lo, "Maritime Commerce and Its Relationship to the Sung Navy," *Journal of the Economic and Social History of the Orient*, vol. 12 (1969), pp. 64–65; 70–72.

46. Ibid., p. 61.

47. Ibid., pp. 62–64.

48. Hudson, "The Medieval Trade of China," in Richards, ed., *Islam and the Trade of Asia*, p. 164.

49. His Chinese name was Pu Luoxin. See Lo, "Maritime Commerce," *Journal of the Economic and Social History of the Orient*, p. 68, and also his "Chinese Shipping," in Mollat, ed., *Sociétés and compagnies*, p. 169.

50. Ibid.

51. Kenneth Hall, "Srivijaya," *Encyclopedia of Asian History* (New York: Charles Scribner's Sons, 1988).

Chapter 3

1. Claude Cahen, "Ikta'," *The Encyclopedia of Islam*, 2nd edn. (Leiden: E. J. Brill, 1960–). Also, E. Ashtor, *A Social and Economic History of the Near East in the Middle Ages* (London: Collins, 1976), pp. 179–180.

2. Marshall G. S. Hodgson, *The Venture of Islam*, vol. 2, *The Expansion of Islam in the Middle Periods* (Chicago: University of Chicago Press, 1974), pp. 402ff.

3. S. D. Goitein, "The Rise of the Near-Eastern Bourgeoisie in Early Islamic Times," *Cahiers d'Histoire Mondiale*, vol. 3 (1957), p. 584.

4. Morris Rossabi, "The Muslims in the Early Yuan Dynasty," in John D. Langlois, ed., *China Under Mongol Rule* (Princeton: Princeton University Press, 1981), pp. 274–275.

5. William H. McNeill, *The Pursuit of Power: Technology, Armed Force and Society Since A.D. 1000* (Oxford: Basil Blackwell, 1983), pp. 43 and 59; D. R. SarDesai, *Southeast Asia, Past and Present*, 2nd edn. (Boulder, CO: Westview Press, 1989), pp. 52–53.

6. Rossabi, "The Muslims in the Early Yuan Dynasty," in Langlois, ed., *China Under Mongol Rule*, pp. 292–293. Marco Polo commented on this hostility toward Muslims: see Jerry H. Bentley, *Old World Encounters: Cross-Cultural Contacts and Exchanges in Pre-Modern Times* (New York: Oxford University Press, 1993), p. 143.

7. Rossabi, "The Muslims in the Early Yuan Dynasty," in Langlois, ed., *China Under Mongol Rule*, p. 275.

8. Leonardo Olschki, *Marco Polo's Asia* (Berkeley: University of California Press, 1960), pp. 232–252.

9. Rossabi, "The Muslims in the Early Yuan Dynasty," in Langlois, ed., *China under Mongol Rule*, p. 283.

10. Ibid., p. 295.

11. Ibid., p. 264.

12. William H. McNeill, *Plagues and Peoples* (Garden City, NY: Anchor Press/ Doubleday, 1976), ch. 4.

13. David Morgan, *Medieval Persia, 1040–1797* (London: Longman, 1988), pp. 84–93.

14. A. S. Ehrenkreutz, "Bahriyya," *The Encyclopedia of Islam*, 2nd edn., Supplement (Leiden: E. J. Brill, 1980).

15. David Ayalon, "Bayriyya," section II, *The Encyclopedia of Islam*, 2nd edn. (Leiden: E. J. Brill, 1960–).

16. Ibid.

17. Ibid.

18. E.g., S. D. Goitein, *Studies in Islamic History and Institutions* (Leiden: E. J. Brill, 1966).

19. S. Y. Labib, "Karimi," *The Encyclopedia of Islam*, 2nd edn. (Leiden: E. J. Brill, 1960–); Ashin Das Gupta, "Indian Merchants and the Trade of the Indian Ocean," in Tapan Raychaudhuri and Irfan Habib, eds., *The Cambridge Economic History of India*, vol. 1, c. 1200–c. 1750 (Cambridge: Cambridge University Press, 1982), pp. 411–412.

20. On Barsbay's limited naval activities, see Ayalon, "Bahriyya," section II, *The Encyclopedia of Islam*, 2nd edn.

21. E. Ashtor, *Levant Trade in the Later Middle Ages* (Princeton: Princeton University Press, 1983), p. 280.

22. Labib, "Karimi," *The Encyclopedia of Islam*, 2nd edn.; also, S. Y. Labib, "Les Marchands Karimis en Orient et sur l'Océan Indien," in Michel Mollat, ed., *Sociétés et compagnies de commerce en Orient et dans l'Océan Indien* (Paris: SEVPEN, 1970), pp. 209–214.

23. Janet Abu-Lughod, *Before European Hegemony: The World System A.D. 1250–1350* (New York: Oxford University Press, 1989), p. 230. See also Michael W. Dols, *The Black Death in the Middle East* (Princeton: Princeton University Press, 1977), pp. 277–280.

24. Ashtor, *Levant Trade*, ch. 1.

25. Stanley Wolpert, *A New History of India*, 4th edn. (New York: Oxford University Press, 1993), pp. 119–120.

26. Burton Stein, "South India: Some General Considerations of the Region and Its Early History," and "Vijayanagar c. 1350–1564," both in Tapan Raychaudhuri and Irfan Habib, eds., *The Cambridge Economic History of India*, vol. 1, c. 1200–c. 1750 (Cambridge: Cambridge University Press, 1982). Cf. Sanjay Subrahmanyam, *The Political Economy of Commerce: Southern India, 1500–1650* (Cambridge: Cambridge University Press, 1990), pp. 340–341. The cavalry horses, often used to fight two Muslim powers (i.e., the Delhi Sultanate and the Bahmani state) were obtained from Central Asia and the Middle East usually through independent Muslim merchants. Geneviève Bouchon, "Les Musulmans du Kerala à l'époque de la découverte portugaise," in Bouchon, *L'Asie du Sud à l'époque Grandes Découvertes* (London: Variorum Reprints, 1987), p. 30.

27. The growth due to birthrate may have had something to do with Islamic law: when foreign Muslim merchants married local women, the resulting chil-

dren were supposed to be brought up as Muslims, following the religion of their father. Growth and expansion were also characteristic of Bengali Muslim communities but they are less well documented. Geneviève Bouchon, "Quelques aspects de l'Islamisation des régions maritimes de l'Inde à l'époque médiévale (XIIe–XVIe siècles)," in Marc Gaborieu, ed., *Islam et Société en Asie du Sud* (Paris: École des Hautes Études en Sciences Sociales, 1986), p. 32.

28. A. A. A. Fyzee, "Bohoras," *The Encyclopedia of Islam*, 2nd edn. (Leiden: E. J. Brill, 1960–). Also, Paul E. Walker, "Bohras," *Encyclopedia of Asian History* (New York: Charles Scribner's Sons, 1988).

29. W. Madelung, "Khodja," *The Encyclopedia of Islam*, 2nd edn. (Leiden: E. J. Brill, 1960–). Also, Paul E. Walker, "Khojas," *Encyclopedia of Asian History* (New York: Charles Scribner's Sons, 1988).

30. Bouchon, "Quelques aspects," in Gaborieu, ed., *Islam et Société*, p. 33.

31. Subrahmanyam, *The Political Economy of Commerce*, ch. 6.

32. Bouchon, "Quelques aspects," in Gaborieu, ed., *Islam et Société*, p. 32.

33. Ibid., pp. 33–34. Also, Bouchon, "Les Musulmans du Kerala," in Bouchon, *L'Asie du Sud à l'époque Grandes Découvertes*, pp. 21–24.

34. Ross E. Dunn, *The Adventures of Ibn Battuta: A Muslim Traveler of the 14th Century* (London: Croom Helm, 1986), pp. 222 and 225.

35. M. N. Pearson, "Calicut," *Encyclopedia of Asian History* (New York: Charles Scribner's Sons, 1988). Geneviève Bouchon, "Un microcosme: Calicut au 16e siècle," in Denys Lombard and Jean Aubin, eds., *Marchands et hommes d'affaires asiatiques dans l'Océan Indien et la Mer de Chine 13e–20e siècles* (Paris: École des Hautes Études en Sciences Sociales, 1988), p. 54.

36. Dunn, *Ibn Battuta*, p. 125.

37. Ibid., pp. 126–127.

38. Ibid., p. 125.

39. John Sutton, *A Thousand Years of East Africa* (Nairobi: British Institute in Eastern Africa, 1990), pp. 63–64.

40. Philip D. Curtin, *Cross-Cultural Trade in World History* (Cambridge: Cambridge University Press, 1984), p. 121.

41. For example, see M. B. Hooker, ed., *Islam in South-East Asia* (Leiden: E. J. Brill, 1983).

42. Abu-Lughod, *Before European Hegemony*, p. 200.

43. McNeill, *The Pursuit of Power*, pp. 44–45.

44. Das Gupta, "Indian Merchants," in Raychaudhuri and Habib, eds., *The Cambridge Economic History of India*, vol. 1, p. 409.

45. G. Coedès, *The Indianized States of Southeast Asia*, ed. by Walter F. Vella and trans. by Susan Brown Cowing (Honolulu: East-West Center Press, 1968), pp. 245–246 and p. 368, n. 97, in which it is explained that Parameshwara might have changed or added to his name, resulting in the identification of two separate rulers. Tomé Pires identifies the convert to Islam as Parameshwara's son. See Tomé Pires, *The Suma Oriental: An Account of the East, from the Red Sea to Japan, written in Malacca and India in 1512–1515*, trans. and ed. by Armando Cortesão (London: The Hakluyt Society, 1944), vol. 2, pp. 239–240. For a slightly different version, see Barbara Watson Andaya and Yoneo Ishii, "Religious Developments in

Southeast Asia, c. 1500–1800," ch. 9 in Nicholas Tarling, ed., *The Cambridge History of Southeast Asia*, vol. 1, *From Early Times to c. 1800* (Cambridge: Cambridge University Press, 1992), p. 516.

46. The chronicle is the *Sejarah Melayu* (Malay Annals). See Kenneth Hall, *Maritime Trade and State Development in Early Southeast Asia* (Honolulu: University of Hawaii Press, 1985), p. 230.

47. Ma Huan, *Ying-Yai Sheng-Lan, "Overall Survey of the Ocean's Shores" (1433)*, trans. and introduced by J. V. G. Mills (Cambridge: The Hakluyt Society, 1970), pp. 108–109. On the Ming expeditions, see Mills' "Introduction," ibid., pp. 1–34, and Harapsad Ray, "China and the 'Western Ocean' in the Fifteenth Century," Satish Chandra, ed., *The Indian Ocean: Explorations in History, Commerce and Politics* (New Delhi: Sage Publications, 1987), pp. 115–119. See also Dianne Lewis, "Melaka," *Encyclopedia of Asian History* (New York: Charles Scribner's Sons, 1988). Not all scholars agree that commerce was a motivation for the Ming expeditions. For example: "Cheng Ho [Zeng He] was an organizer, a commander, a diplomat, and an able courtier, but he was not a trader. No chartered companies grew out of his expeditions." Noted in John K. Fairbank and Edwin O. Reischauer, *China: Tradition and Transformation*, revised edn. (Boston: Houghton Mifflin Co., 1989), p. 199.

48. Coedès, *The Indianized States of Southeast Asia*, p. 245.

49. Hall, *Maritime Trade*, pp. 215, 226–228, 230. See also C. Wake, "Malacca's Early Kings and the Reception of Islam," *Journal of Southeast Asian History*, vol. 2 (1964), pp. 104–128.

50. Luis Filipe Thomaz, "The Malay Sultanate of Melaka," in Anthony Reid, ed., *Southeast Asia in the Early Modern Era: Trade, Power and Belief?* (Ithaca, NY: Cornell University Press, 1993), pp. 75 and 77.

51. Tomé Pires, *Suma*, vol. 2, p. 273. Later, the Portuguese were charged a high ten percent. Thomaz, "The Malay Sultanate," in Reid, ed., *Southeast Asia*, pp. 74, 78, and 87.

52. Thomaz discusses the higher estimates in ibid., p. 71. The lower figure is accepted by M. A. P. Meilink-Roelofsz, "Trade and Islam in the Malay-Indonesian Archipelago Prior to the Arrival of the Europeans," in D. S. Richards, ed., *Islam and the Trade of Asia* (Oxford: Bruno Cassirer, 1970), p. 150.

53. Luis Filipe Thomaz, "Malaka et ses communautés marchandes au tournant du 16e siècle," in Denys Lombard and Jean Aubin, eds., *Marchands et hommes d'affaires asiatiques dans l'Océan Indien et la Mer de Chine, 13e–20e siècles* (Paris: École des Hautes Études en Sciences Sociales, 1988), pp. 37–39.

54. "Malacca cannot live without Cambay, nor Cambay without Malacca, if they are to be very rich and prosperous," Tomé Pires, *Suma*, vol. 1, p. 45.

55. K. N. Chaudhuri, *Trade and Civilisation in the Indian Ocean: An Economic History from the Rise of Islam to 1750* (Cambridge: Cambridge University Press, 1985), p. 109.

56. M. A. P. Meilink-Roelofsz, *Asian Trade and European Influence in the Indonesian Archipelago Between 1500 and About 1630* (The Hague: Martinus Nijhoff, 1962), p. 25; Rita Rose Di Meglio, "Arab Trade with Indonesia and the Malay Peninsula from the 8th to the 16th Century," in D. S. Richards, ed., *Islam and the Trade of Asia* (Oxford: Bruno Cassirer, 1970), p. 122.

57. On preference for local law, see Thomaz, "The Malay Sultanate," in Reid, ed., *Southeast Asia,* p. 79.

58. Shihab al-din Ahmad ibn Majid, quoted in translation by G. R. Tibbetts, *A Study of the Arabic Texts Containing Material on South-East Asia* (Leiden: E. J. Brill, 1979), p. 206. See also Thomaz, "The Malay Sultanate," in Reid, ed., *Southeast Asia,* p. 79. Ibn Majid is identified as the pilot hired by Vasco da Gama: see S. Maqbul Ahmad, "Ibn Madjid," *The Encyclopedia of Islam,* 2nd edn. (Leiden: E. J. Brill, 1960–).

59. Thomaz, "The Malay Sultanate," in Reid, ed., *Southeast Asia,* pp. 80, 88–89.

60. There is extensive material on Arabization and Islamization. An example for Southeast Asia: Anthony Reid, *Southeast Asia in the Age of Commerce, 1450–1680,* 2 vols.: vol. 1, *The Lands Below the Winds* (New Haven: Yale University Press, 1988); vol. 2, *Expansion and Crisis* (New Haven: Yale University Press, 1993). An example for East Africa: J. Spencer Trimingham, *Islam in East Africa* (Oxford: Clarendon Press, 1964).

61. Curtin, *Cross-Cultural Trade,* ch. 6; Abu-Lughod, *Before European Hegemony,* p. 275; Chaudhuri, *Trade and Civilisation,* p. 14; Archibald Lewis, "Maritime Skills in the Indian Ocean, 1368–1500," *Journal of the Economic and Social History of the Orient,* vol. 16, parts 2 and 3 (1973), p. 264. A source often cited in support of the contention about peaceful trade in the pre-European era is Auguste Toussaint, *History of the Indian Ocean,* trans. by June Guicharnaud (Chicago: University of Chicago Press, 1966), p. 101: "Until the arrival of the Portuguese, the Indian Ocean had never been the theatre of very serious conflicts. Doubtless piracy had always been fairly active there, ... but all that was sham fighting compared to the raging battles that closely followed the first Portuguese expedition."

62. The geographical foci of her eight links or circuits are: East Asia with Southeast Asia; the Silk Road; the Bay of Bengal with its littorals; the Arabian Sea with its littorals; the Persian Gulf region; the Red Sea region; the Mediterranean Sea region; Europe. See Abu-Lughod, *Before European Hegemony,* p. 34, figure 1.

63. Elizabeth Endicott-West, review of Abu-Lughod's book, *The Journal of Asian Studies,* vol. 49, no. 2 (May, 1990), pp. 349–350. Endicott-West points out that Mongol civil wars interrupted trade during the so-called *Pax Mongolica.*

64. In *Before European Hegemony,* Abu-Lughod allocates approximately 90 pages to Europe, 30 to non-Muslim South Asia and Southeast Asia, 35 to China, and 145 to the Islamic areas of South and Southeast Asia and the Middle East combined. Her analysis rests heavily on the Islamic contributions to the system.

65. Fernand Braudel, *Civilization and Capitalism, 15th–18th Century,* trans. by Sian Reynolds (New York: Harper and Row, 1982–1984); Immanuel Wallerstein, *The Modern World System* (New York: Academic Press, 1974–).

66. Abu-Lughod, *Before European Hegemony,* pp. 364 and 369–372.

67. Immanuel Wallerstein, review of Abu-Lughod's book, *International Journal of Middle East Studies,* vol. 24, no. 1 (Feb., 1992), pp. 128–131. There is some disagreement between the two scholars on how to define a world system.

68. Niels Steensgaard, "The Indian Ocean Network and the Emerging World-Economy, c. 1500–1750," in Satish Chandra, ed., *The Indian Ocean: Explorations in History, Commerce and Politics* (New Delhi: Sage Publications, 1987), p. 127.

69. Wallerstein, review of Abu-Lughod's book, *International Journal of Middle East Studies*, p. 129. See also McNeill, *The Pursuit of Power*, ch. 2.

70. Simon Digby, "The Maritime Trade of India," in Tapan Raychaudhuri and Irfan Habib, eds., *The Cambridge Economic History of India*, vol. 1, c. 1200–c. 1750 (Cambridge: Cambridge University Press, 1982), pp. 152–154.

71. SarDesai, *Southeast Asia*, p. 42; O. W. Wolters, *Early Indonesian Commerce* (Ithaca, NY: Cornell University Press, 1967), pp. 238–239 and 252.

72. Goitein, *Studies*, p. 348; also his *A Mediterranean Society*, vol. 1, *Economic Foundations* (Berkeley: University of California Press, 1967), pp. 327–332.

73. Dunn, *Ibn Battuta*, p. 219; Digby, "The Maritime Trade of India," in Raychaudhuri and Habib, eds., *The Cambridge Economic History of India*, vol. 1, p. 152. There were also good reasons for *unarmed* convoy, such as sailing in the off-season when the weather could be more dangerous than usual or in the case that a vessel was in poor condition. See R. B. Serjeant, "Maritime Customary Law Off the Arabian Coasts," in Michel Mollat, ed., *Sociétés et compagnies de commerce en Orient et dans l'Océan Indien* (Paris: SEVPEN, 1970), pp. 199–201.

74. Digby, "The Maritime Trade of India," in Raychaudhuri and Habib, eds., *The Cambridge Economic History of India*, vol. 1, pp. 152–153.

75. Dunn, *Ibn Battuta*, pp. 246–247.

76. Reid, *Southeast Asia in the Age of Commerce*, vol. 2, pp. 220–221.

77. Dunn, *Ibn Battuta*, p. 249.

78. Hodgson, *The Venture of Islam*, vol. 2, p. 541.

79. Pamela Gutman, "Arakan," *Encyclopedia of Asian History* (New York: Charles Scribner's Sons, 1988). This occurred in the fifteenth and sixteenth centuries.

80. Duarte Barbosa, *The Book of Duarte Barbosa: An Account of the Countries Bordering on the Indian Ocean and Their Inhabitants, Written by Duarte Barbosa, and Completed in About the Year 1518 A.D.*, trans. and ed. by Mansel Longworth Dames (London: The Hakluyt Society, 1918–1920), vol. 2, pp. 171–172.

Chapter 4

1. Niels Steensgaard, *The Asian Trade Revolution of the Seventeenth Century* (Chicago: University of Chicago Press, 1974). The original title of the book had more modest implications: *Carracks, Caravans and Companies: The Structural Crisis in the European-Asian Trade in the Early 17th Century* (Copenhagen: Scandinavian Institute of Asian Studies, 1972).

2. Immanuel Wallerstein, "The Incorporation of the Indian Subcontinent into the Capitalist World-Economy," in Satish Chandra, ed., *The Indian Ocean: Explorations in History, Commerce and Politics* (New Delhi: Sage Publications, 1987).

3. Blair B. Kling and M. N. Pearson, eds., *The Age of Partnership: Europeans in Asia Before Dominion* (Honolulu: University of Hawaii Press, 1979). This collection of essays was published in honor of Holden Furber, to whom the idea of Asian-European partnership is credited. See Sanjay Subrahmanyam, *The Political Economy of Commerce: South India, 1500–1650* (Cambridge: Cambridge University Press, 1990), p. 252, including note 1.

4. E.g., M. N. Pearson, *Before Colonialism: Theories on Asian-European Relations 1500–1750* (Delhi: Oxford University Press, 1988), pp. 10, 25–27.

5. E.g., Stanford J. Shaw, *History of the Ottoman Empire and Modern Turkey*, vol. 1, *Empire of the Gazis: The Rise and Decline of the Ottoman Empire, 1280–1808* (Cambridge: Cambridge University Press, 1976), pp. 291–292, on the ideas of Katip Çelebi. Also, Norman Itzkowitz, *Ottoman Empire and Islamic Tradition* (Chicago: University of Chicago Press, Phoenix Edition, 1980), p. 88.

6. Shaw, *History of the Ottoman Empire*, vol. 1, pp. 107 and 147.

7. Andrew Hess, "The Evolution of the Ottoman Seaborne Empire in the Age of Oceanic Discoveries, 1453–1525," *The American Historical Review*, vol. 75 (Dec., 1970), p. 1914.

8. On the Shi'i imamate, see Chapter 2 of this volume. The Safavid Isma'il should not be confused with the seventh imam recognized by Isma'ili Shi'i Muslims.

9. Much of early Shi'i martyrdom history is associated with locations in Iraq, especially Karbala; such places became destinations of Shi'i pilgrimage. See, e.g., Husain M. Jafri, *Origins and Early Development of Shi'a Islam* (London: Longman Group Ltd., 1979), ch. 7.

10. An overview of the policies of Shah Abbas is given in Jean Calmard, "Les marchands iraniens," in Denys Lombard and Jean Aubin, eds., *Marchands et hommes d'affaires asiatiques dans l'Océan Indien et la Mer de Chine 13e–20e siècles* (Paris: Écoles des Hautes Études en Science Sociales, 1988), p. 99. On contact with Europeans, see Roger Savory, *Iran Under the Safavids* (Cambridge: Cambridge University Press, 1980), ch. 5 and pp. 192–202.

11. Steensgaard, *Asian Trade Revolution*, e.g., pp. 104–110.

12. Cf. Calmard, "Les merchands iraniens," in Lombard and Aubin, eds., *Marchands et hommes d'affaires asiatiques*, pp. 94, 99.

13. For a general history of the Mughals, Akbar through Aurangzeb, see Stanley Wolpert, *A New History of India*, 4th edn. (New York: Oxford University Press, 1993), chs. 9 and 11.

14. Ashin Das Gupta, "Indian Merchants and the Trade in the Indian Ocean," in Tapan Raychaudhuri and Irfan Habib, eds., *The Cambridge Economic History of India*, vol. 1, c. 1200–c. 1750 (Cambridge: Cambridge University Press, 1982), p. 426.

15. Geneviève Bouchon, "Sixteenth Century Malabar and the Indian Ocean," in Ashin Das Gupta and M. N. Pearson, eds., *India and the Indian Ocean, 1500–1800* (Calcutta: Oxford University Press, 1987), p. 182. More detailed information is given in another Bouchon article, "Pour une histoire du Gujarat du XVe au XVIIe siècle," in Bouchon, *L'Asie du Sud à l'époque des Grandes Découvertes* (London: Variorum Reprints, 1987), p. 149.

16. Holden Furber, *Rival Empires of Trade in the Orient, 1600–1800* (Minneapolis: University of Minnesota Press, 1976), p. 15.

17. John F. Richards, *The New Cambridge History of India*, part 1, vol. 5, *The Mughal Empire* (Cambridge: Cambridge University Press, 1993), pp. 228 and 199.

18. Niels Steensgaard, "The Indian Ocean Network and the Emerging World-Economy, c. 1500–1750," in Satish Chandra, ed., *The Indian Ocean: Explorations*

in History, Commerce and Politics (New Delhi: Sage Publications, 1987), pp. 137–138; Furber, *Rival Empires of Trade*, p. 93.

19. A contrasting, non-Mughal example of state policy that affected maritime trade: a local ruler's attempt to monopolize the production and export of Travancore's Malabar pepper in the 1730s, partly to thwart the Dutch. See Das Gupta, "Indian Merchants," in Raychaudhuri and Habib, eds., *The Cambridge Economic History of India*, vol. 1, p. 422.

20. C. A. Bayly, "India and West Asia, c. 1700–1830," *Asian Affairs*, vol. 19, no. 1 (Feb., 1988), p. 11.

21. Subrahmanyam, *The Political Economy of Commerce*, pp. 367–368.

22. John E. Wills, Jr., "Maritime China from Wang Chih to Shih Lang: Themes in Peripheral History," in Jonathan D. Spence and John E. Wills, Jr., eds., *From Ming to Ch'ing: Conquest, Region, and Continuity in Seventeenth-Century China* (New Haven: Yale University Press, 1979), p. 204. Also, G. B. Souza, "Maritime Trade and Politics in China and the South China Sea," in Ashin Das Gupta and M. N. Pearson, *India and the Indian Ocean, 1500–1800* (Calcutta: Oxford University Press, 1987), pp. 319, 321.

23. Anthony Reid, *Southeast Asia in the Age of Commerce, 1450–1680*, 2 vols., vol. 2, *Expansion and Crisis* (New Haven: Yale University Press, 1993), pp. 316 and 122. The same was true of "turning Malay." See Barbara Watson Andaya and Yoneo Ishii, "Religious Developments in Southeast Asia, c. 1500–1800," ch. 9 in Nicholas Tarling, ed., *The Cambridge History of Southeast Asia*, vol. 1, *From Early Times to c. 1800* (Cambridge: Cambridge University Press, 1992), p. 517.

24. S. Arasaratnam, "India and the Indian Ocean in the Seventeenth Century," in Ashin Das Gupta and M. N. Pearson, *India and the Indian Ocean, 1500–1800* (Calcutta: Oxford University Press, 1987), p. 120.

25. Morris Rossabi, "Muslim and Central Asian Revolts," in Jonathan D. Spence and John E Wills, Jr., eds., *From Ming to Ch'ing: Conquest, Region, and Continuity in Seventeenth-Century China* (New Haven: Yale University Press, 1979), pp. 179–181.

26. Joseph F. Fletcher, "China and Central Asia, 1368–1884," in John K. Fairbank, ed., *The Chinese World Order* (Cambridge, MA: Harvard University Press, 1968), pp. 209–210. Also, David Morgan, *Medieval Persia 1040–1797* (London: Longman, 1988), p. 91.

27. Rossabi, "Muslim and Central Asian Revolts," in Spence and Wills, eds., *From Ming to Ch'ing*, pp. 182–183.

28. Ibid., p. 191.

29. Ibid., p. 193. Also, Fletcher, "China and Central Asia," in Fairbank, ed., *The Chinese World Order*, pp. 223–224. Also, for "New Sect" Islamic rebellions of the eighteenth and nineteenth centuries, in the northwest and in Yunnan province, the aim of which was the establishment of Islamic states, see R. Israeli, "Islamization and Sinicization in Chinese Islam," in Nehemia Levtzion, ed., *Conversion to Islam* (New York: Holmes & Meier Publishers, Inc., 1979).

30. William S. Atwell, "A Seventeenth-Century 'General Crisis' in East Asia?" *Modern Asian Studies*, vol. 24, no. 4 (1990), esp. pp. 671–673; Jack A. Goldstone, "East and West in the Seventeenth Century: Political Crises in Stuart England,

Ottoman Turkey, and Ming China," *Comparative Studies in Society and History*, vol. 30, no. 1 (Jan., 1988), pp. 106–110.

31. Ibid., pp. 120–126.

32. Bayly, "India and West Asia," *Asian Affairs*, vol. 19, no. 1 (Feb., 1988). His point is that the suppression of unruly groups was part of the mechanism used by the British to establish power in Asia.

33. J. van Leur, *Indonesian Trade and Society: Essays in Asian Social and Economic History* (The Hague: W. van Hoeve, 1955), e.g., pp. 135–136, 197–200. Philip D. Curtin, *Cross-Cultural Trade in World History* (Cambridge: Cambridge University Press, 1984), p. 134.

34. Steensgaard, *The Asian Trade Revolution*, pp. 28ff. K. N. Chaudhuri, *Trade and Civilisation in the Indian Ocean: An Economic History from the Rise of Islam to 1750* (Cambridge: Cambridge University Press, 1985), ch. 10.

35. Maxime Rodinson, *Islam and Capitalism*, trans. by Brian Pearce (Austin: University of Texas Press, 1978), p. 40, citing the seventeen-century traveler John Chardin; Reid, *Southeast Asia in the Age of Commerce*, vol. 2, p. 111. On sarrafs, see also Chapter 2 in this volume, in text at note 22.

36. At Muslim ports, such an official had one of a number of titles, depending on the culture and the job description. In South Arabian ports, he might be *amir al-bahr*, "commander of the sea." In the many ports where Persian was the first language of trade, in the Gulf region and in India, he might be *shahbandar* or *malik-i tujjar*, literally, "shah of the port" or "king of the merchants." Another similar title was *ra'is*, "chief," an Arabic word that was used in Ottoman Turkish to denote naval rank. Four shahbandars were reported at Melaka, dividing among them four major regions from which merchants came. Arun Das Gupta, "The Maritime Trade of Indonesia: 1500–1800," in Ashin Das Gupta and M. N. Pearson, eds., *India and the Indian Ocean, 1500–1800*, p. 249.

37. M. A. P. Meilink-Roelofsz, "Trade and Islam in the Malay-Indonesian Archipelago Prior to the Arrival of the Europeans," in D. S. Richards, ed., *Islam and the Trade of Asia* (Oxford: Bruno Cassirer, 1970), p. 152. K. N. Chaudhuri, *The Trading World of Asia and the English East India Company, 1660–1760* (Cambridge: Cambridge University Press, 1978), pp. 136–138.

38. Ashin Das Gupta, "A Note on the Shipowning Merchants of Surat c. 1700," in Denys Lombard and Jean Aubin, eds., *Marchands et hommes d'affaires asiatiques dans l'Océan Indien et la Mer de Chine 13e–20e siècles* (Paris: École des Hautes Études en Sciences Sociales, 1988), p. 109.

39. Chaudhuri, *Trade and Civilisation*, pp. 209–210; also his *The Trading World of Asia*, pp. 136–138.

40. The fourteenth-century philosopher of history, Ibn Khaldun, discusses merchant capitalism in *The Muqaddimah: An Introduction to History*, trans. Franz Rosenthal, ed. and abridged by N. J. Dawood (Princeton: Princeton University Press, 1967), e.g., p. 298. On types of capitalism, see Chaudhuri, *Trade and Civilisation*, ch. 10; Pearson, *Before Colonialism*. Cf. Subrahmanyam, *The Political Economy of Commerce*, pp. 327–339.

41. Reid, *Southeast Asia in the Age of Commerce*, vol. 2: for Muslim military expansion in island Southeast Asia, especially Java, see pp. 169–176; for the mainland, see pp. 186–192; see also pp. 182 and 212–214.

42. Andaya and Ishii, "Religious Developments," in Tarling, ed., *The Cambridge History of Southeast Asia,* vol. 1, pp. 519–520.

43. Ibid., pp. 173–174. See also Chapter 3 of this volume, in text after note 44.

44. E.g., Lea E. Williams, *Southeast Asia: A History* (New York: Oxford University Press, 1976), p. 43.

45. E.g., Robert Stevens, *The New and Complete Guide to the East India Trade* (London, 1775), p. 128: At Muscat, "Mahometans pay ... 2 and 1/2 per Cent. And all other Nations pay ... 5 ditto." Stevens does not provide comprehensive or consistent evidence on customs rates. For the same rates in the Ottoman Empire, see Bruce Masters, *The Origins of Western Economic Dominance in the Middle East: Mercantilism and the Islamic Economy in Aleppo, 1600–1750* (New York: New York University Press, 1988), p. 138.

46. For an example, see Chapter 5 of this volume, section on Tipu Sultan. The differences between commercial and political agents was not always sharply defined, but distinctive terms are used in the sources, e.g., *dallal* for broker; *wakil* or *darogha* for political agent.

47. E.g., Muscati control over East African ports through an appanage system. See P. Risso, *Oman and Muscat: An Early Modern History* (London: Croom Helm and New York: St. Martin's Press, 1986), ch. 7.

48. Curtin, *Cross-Cultural Trade,* esp. ch. 1.

49. Michel Aghassian and Kéram Kévonian, "Le commerce arménien dans l'Océan Indien aux 17e et 18e siècles," in Denys Lombard and Jean Aubin, eds., *Marchands et hommes d'affaires asiatiques dan l'Océan Indien et la Mer de Chine 13e–20e siècles* (Paris: École des Hautes Études en Sciences Sociales, 1988), pp. 155–158. Also, John Carswell, "The Armenians and East-West Trade Through Persia in the XVIIth Century," in Michel Mollat, ed., *Sociétés et compagnies de commerce en Orient et dans l'Océan Indien* (Paris: SEVPEN, 1970), pp. 481–486.

50. Lvon Khachikian, "The Ledger of the Merchant Hovannes Joughayetsi," *Journal of the Asiatic Society,* vol. 8, no. 3 (1966), pp. 153–186. Armenians had a reputation for being diligent linguists. Armenians trading *to* Isfahan could count on a number of Armenians there to know Turkish and Persian. Carswell, "The Armenians and East-West Trade," in Mollat, ed., *Sociétés et compagnies,* p. 482.

51. E. g., Subrahmanyam, *The Political Economy of Commerce,* pp. 371–373. For other examples, see Stevens, *The New and Complete Guide,* passim. Such diversity also characterized pre-modern European trade. See Chaudhuri, *The Trading World of Asia,* p. 138.

52. Jean Aubin, "Marchands de Mer Rouge et du Golfe Persique au tournant des 15e et 16e siècles," in Denys Lombard and Jean Aubin, eds., *Marchands et hommes d'affaires asiatiques dans l'Océan Indien et la Mer de Chine 13e–20e siècles* (Paris: École des Hautes Études en Sciences Sociales, 1988), pp. 89–90.

53. Hamid Algar, "Kazaruni," *The Encyclopedia of Islam,* 2nd edn. (Leiden: E. J. Brill, 1960–); J. Spencer Trimingham, *The Sufi Orders of Islam* (London: Oxford University Press, 1973), pp. 236 and 20–21. Trimingham argues that the Kazaruniyya was simply a group and not a true "way" (*tariqa*) because it had no distinctive teachings.

54. Gilbert Hamonic, "Les réseaux marchands bugis-makassar," in Denys Lombard and Jean Aubin, eds., *Marchands et hommes d'affaires asiatiques dans*

l'Océan Indien et la Mer de Chine 13e–20e siècles (Paris: École des Hautes Études en Sciences Sociales, 1988), p. 262.

55. André Raymond, *Artisans et commerçants au Caire au XVIIIe siècle* (Damascus: Institut français de Damas, 1973–1974), vol. 1, pp. 126–127, citing De Maillet.

56. Chaudhuri, *The Trading World of Asia*, p. 150. Chaudhuri comments that this was not an isolated incident. He uses it as an example of religious exclusivity.

57. Calvin H. Allen, "Sayyids, Shets, and Sultans: Politics of Trade in Masqat under the Al bu Saʻid, 1785–1914." Unpubl. Ph.D. disseration, University of Washington (Seattle), 1978, p. 105. See also Allen, "The Indian Merchant Community of Masqat," *Bulletin of the School of Oriental and African Studies*, v. 44 (1981), p. 42.

58. On the companies and their employees, see Furber, *Rival Empires of Trade*, and L. Blussé and F. Gaastra, eds., *Companies and Trade: Essays on Overseas Trading Companies During the Ancien Régime* (Leiden: Leiden University Press, 1981).

59. Chaudhuri, *The Trading World of Asia*, pp. 314–317 and 198–199. One curious impact that European presence had was to encourage the use and abuse of national flags. Both Asian and European vessels could hoist colors other than their own in order to claim the protection of a stronger state or to avoid seizure by fooling potential enemies. For an example, see ibid., p. 199.

60. Stevens, *The New and Complete Guide*, p. 128.

61. K. Glamann, *Dutch-Asiatic Trade, 1620–1740* (Copenhagen, 1958), p. 192.

62. Barbara Watson Andaya, *Perak, the Abode of Grace* (Kuala Lumpur: Oxford University Press, 1979), p. 80.

63. Ibid., pp. 79 and 106.

64. Risso, *Oman*, p. 201.

65. Carswell, "The Armenians and East-West Trade," in Mollat, ed., *Sociétés et compagnies*, p. 484.

66. Chaudhuri, *The Trading World of Asia*, pp. 223–224; another example involved the use of British broadcloth for Mughal military uniforms: ibid., p. 223.

67. Glamann, *Dutch-Asiatic Trade*, pp. 206–211.

68. Risso, *Oman*, pp. 194–200.

69. Ibid., p. 146.

70. Ibid., p. 160, n. 18.

71. Ibid., p. 152.

Chapter 5

1. Philip D. Curtin, *Cross-Cultural Trade in World History* (Cambridge: Cambridge University Press, 1984), p. 136.

2. Ibid., p. 149.

3. C. R. Boxer, *The Portuguese Seaborne Empire, 1415–1825* (New York: Alfred A. Knopf, 1969), pp. 19 and 33.

4. Sanjay Subrahmanyam, *The Political Economy of Commerce: Southern India, 1500–1650* (Cambridge: Cambridge University Press, 1990), p. 103.

5. D. R. SarDesai, *Southeast Asia: Past and Present*, 2nd edn. (Boulder, CO: Westview Press, 1989), p. 62. Boxer, *The Portuguese Seaborne Empire*, p. 305,

quotes an Italian Jesuit, writing in 1550, complaining about slavery among the Portuguese at Melaka, especially sexual slavery. For Ibn Majid's comments, see Chapter 3, of this volume, in text, at note 58.

6. Subrahmanyam, *The Political Economy of Commerce*, pp. 105–106.

7. M. N. Pearson, "Merchants and States," in James D. Tracy, ed., *The Political Economy of Merchant Empires* (Cambridge: Cambridge University Press, 1991), p. 79.

8. M. N. Pearson, *Merchants and Rulers in Gujarat: The Response to the Portuguese in the Sixteenth Century* (Berkeley: University of California Press, 1976), pp. 93–96. Also, Subrahmanyam, *The Political Economy of Commerce*, p. 108. In the second half of the sixteenth century, the Portuguese tried a concession scheme: in exchange for service to the crown, a private merchant could obtain rights over a commercial voyage between two ports in the Indian Ocean. These may have been more effective than the cartaz system in imposing monopoly conditions. Ibid., pp. 112–113.

9. Curtin, *Cross-Cultural Trade*, p. 142.

10. Two Portuguese holdings lasted into the twentieth century. Goa became part of the Republic of India in 1961. Macao is due to join the People's Republic of China in 1999.

11. Curtin, *Cross-Cultural Trade*, pp. 150–151.

12. Geneviève Bouchon, "Pour une histoire du Gujarat du XVe au XVIIe siècle," in her *L'Asie du Sud à l'époque des Grandes Découvertes* (London: Variorum Reprints, 1987), p. 153.

13. Coen quoted by Niels Steensgaard, "The Indian Ocean Network and the Emerging World-Economy, c. 1500–1750," in Satish Chandra, ed., *The Indian Ocean Explorations in History, Commerce and Politics* (New Delhi: Sage Publications, 1987), 139.

14. Arun Das Gupta, "The Maritime Trade of Indonesia: 1500–1800," in Ashin Das Gupta and M. N. Pearson, eds., *India and the Indian Ocean, 1500–1800* (Calcutta: Oxford University Press, 1987), p. 252, in part, citing C. R. Boxer.

15. Neils Steensgaard, *The Asian Trade Revolution of the Seventeenth Century* (Chicago: University of Chicago Press, 1974), esp. chs. 3 and 4. In addition to structure Steensgaard also pays considerable attention to events and diplomacy: chs. 5–7.

16. Bruce Masters, *The Origins of Western Economic Dominance in the Middle East: Mercantilism and the Islamic Economy in Aleppo, 1600–1750* (New York: New York University Press, 1988), p. 216.

17. Ibid., pp. 193–197.

18. Om Prakash, "The Dutch East India Company in the Trade of the Indian Ocean," in Ashin Das Gupta and M. N. Pearson, eds., *India and the Indian Ocean, 1500–1800* (Calcutta: Oxford University Press, 1987), p. 189 and note 5.

19. Lea E. Williams, *Southeast Asia: A History* (New York: Oxford University Press, 1976), ch. 4.

20. P. Risso, *Oman and Muscat: An Early Modern History* (London: Croom Helm and New York: St. Martin's Press, 1986), pp. 80 and 83.

21. P. Risso [Dubuisson], "Qasimi Piracy and the General Treaty of Peace (1820)," *Arabian Studies*, vol. 4 (1978).

22. In the seventeenth century, the English had sought an establishment at Muscat without success. R. D. Bathurst, "The Ya'rubi Dynasty of Oman," unpublished DPhil dissertation, Oxford University, 1967, pp. 164–167.

23. *Correspondance inédite officielle et confidentielle de Napoléon Bonaparte avec les cours étrangères* (Paris, 1809–1820), vol. 6, book 4, "Egypte."

24. Risso, *Oman,* p. 154, citing India Office Records, London (hereafter, IOR), Bombay Political and Secret Proceedings, Range 381, vol. 16, p. 5901.

25. Risso, *Oman,* p. 145, citing IOR, Bombay State Papers, Select Consultations, Range E, vol. 10, pp. 857–859, for July 1796.

26. Risso, *Oman,* p. 145.

27. Ibid., p. 157.

28. Calvin H. Allen, Jr., "The State of Masqat in the Gulf and East Africa, 1785–1829," *International Journal of Middle East Studies,* vol. 14, no. 2 (May, 1982), pp. 124–125.

29. Calvin H. Allen, Jr., "The Indian Merchant Community of Masqat," *Bulletin of the School of Oriental and African Studies,* vol. 44 (1981), pp. 48–51. W. Madelung, "Khodja," *The Encyclopedia of Islam,* 2nd edn. (Leiden: E. J. Brill, 1960–).

30. Calvin H. Allen, "Sayyids, Shets and Sultans: Politics and Trade in Masqat Under the Al Bu Sa'id, 1785–1914," unpublished PhD dissertation, University of Washington, 1978, pp. 140–157.

31. Ibid., pp. 124–126 and 112.

32. Dietmar Rothermund, *Asian Trade and European Expansion in the Age of Mercantilism* (New Delhi: Manohar, 1981), p. x.

33. T. K. Derry and Trevor I. Williams, *A Short History of Technology from the Earliest Times to A.D. 1900* (Oxford: Clarendon Press, 1960), pp. 364–373.

34. S. Bhattacharya, "The Indian Ocean in the Nineteenth and Early Twentieth Centuries," in Satish Chandra, *The Indian Ocean: Explorations in History, Commerce and Politics* (New Delhi: Sage Publications, 1987), p. 305.

35. For the impact of the steamship on Gulf trade, see R. G. Landen, *Oman Since 1856: Disruptive Modernization in a Traditional Arab Society* (Princeton: Princeton University Press, 1967), ch. 3; on Indian involvement, p. 102.

36. On this designation, see Stephen Frederic Dale, "Mappilas," *Encyclopedia of Asian History* (New York: Charles Scribner's Sons, 1988).

37. See Chapter 3 of this volume, in text at notes 32 and 33.

38. Geneviève Bouchon, "Un microcosme: Calicut au 16e siècle," in Denys Lombard and Jean Aubin, *Marchands et hommes d'affaires asiatiques dans l'Océan Indien et la Mer de Chine 13e–20e siècles* (Paris: École des Hautes Études en Sciences Sociales, 1988), p. 50.

39. M. N. Pearson, "India and the Indian Ocean in the Sixteenth Century," in Ashin Das Gupta and M. N. Pearson, eds., *India and the Indian Ocean, 1500–1800* (Calcutta: Oxford University Press, 1987), p. 82.

40. Geneviève Bouchon, "Sixteenth Century Malabar and the Indian Ocean," in Ashin Das Gupta and M. N. Pearson, eds., *India and the Indian Ocean, 1500–1800* (Calcutta: Oxford University Press, 1987).

41. Ibid., p. 179. On the Portuguese period of Mappila history, see also Stephen Frederic Dale, *Islamic Society on the South Asian Frontier: The Mappilas of Malabar, 1498–1922* (Oxford: Clarendon Press, 1980), chs. 1 and 2.

42. S. Arasaratnam, "India and the Indian Ocean in the Seventeenth Century," in Ashin Das Gupta and M. N. Pearson, eds., *India and the Indian Ocean, 1500–1800* (Calcutta: Oxford University Press, 1987), pp. 114–115.

43. SarDesai, *Southeast Asia*, p. 59.

44. Subrahmanyam, *The Political Economy of Commerce*, pp. 47, 82, 89. On an Iranian-born merchant-general who dominated Masulipatnam in the 1640s, see ibid., pp. 322–327. On Masulipatnam, see Chapter 4 of this volume, in text at note 17.

45. Golconda came under Mughal rule in the late seventeenth century but became independent again in the eighteenth. Holden Furber, *Rival Empires of Trade in the Orient, 1600–1800* (Minneapolis: University of Minnesota Press, 1976), pp. 11–12.

46. Anthony Reid, "Islamization and Christianization in Southeast Asia: The Critical Phase, 1550–1650," in Anthony Reid, ed., *Southeast Asia in the Early Modern Era: Trade, Power and Belief* (Ithaca, NY: Cornell University Press, 1993), p. 162.

47. Ibid., pp. 160–163 and 176–179.

48. Ibid., p. 165, including notes 44 and 45. Cf. Anthony Reid, *Southeast Asia in the Age of Commerce, 1450–1680*, 2 vols., vol. 2 *Expansion and Crisis* (New Haven: Yale University Press, 1993), p. 147.

49. Pierre-Yves Manguin, "The Vanishing *Jong:* Insular Southeast Asian Fleets in Trade and War (Fifteenth to Seventeenth Centuries)," in Anthony Reid, ed., *Southeast Asia in the Early Modern Era: Trade, Power and Belief* (Ithaca, NY: Cornell University Press, 1993), p. 205.

50. A. J. Piekaar, "Atjeh," second section of entry, *The Encyclopedia of Islam*, 2nd edn. (Leiden: E. J. Brill, 1960–), esp. p. 744.

51. For a contemporary, largely negative appraisal of Tipu Sultan, see commentary in William Kirkpatrick, ed. and trans., *Select Letters of Tippoo Sultan* (London, 1811). For a positive revisionist view, see Mohibbul Hasan, *History of Tipu Sultan*, 2nd edn. (Calcutta: The World Press Private Ltd., 1971).

52. On the popular controversy see, for example, Barbara Crossette, "Sultan Died a Hero, but His Name Is Now Sullied in a Religious Dispute," *The New York Times*, February 1, 1990, p. A4.

53. Tipu Sultan to the Padshah, 23 June 1785, in Kirkpatrick, ed. and trans., *Select Letters of Tippoo Sultan*, letter LXXI. Parentheses are Kirkpatrick's, brackets are mine.

54. Ralph Austen, "The 19th Century Islamic Slave Trade from East Africa (Swahili and Red Sea Coasts): A Tentative Census," in William Gervase Clarence-Smith, ed., *The Economics of the Indian Ocean Slave Trade in the Nineteenth Century* (London: Frank Cass, 1989), e.g., p. 26. Curiously, abolitionist estimates have been construed as an "assault on Islam." Ibid., p. 21.

55. Bernard Lewis, *Race and Slavery in the Middle East: An Historical Inquiry* (Oxford: Oxford University Press, 1992), ch. 14.

56. A. Sheriff, "Localisation and Social Composition of the East African Slave Trade, 1858–1873," in William Gervase Clarence-Smith, ed., *The Economics of the Indian Ocean Slave Trade in the Nineteenth Century* (London: Frank Cass, 1989), p. 131. Also, Austen, "The 19th Century Islamic Slave Trade," in Clarence-Smith, ed., *The Economics of the Indian Ocean Slave Trade*, p. 22.

57. E.g., Anthony Reid, "Introduction: Slavery and Bondage in Southeast Asian History," in Anthony Reid, ed., *Slavery, Bondage and Dependency in Southeast Asia* (New York: St. Martin's Press, 1983). South Asian and Burmese slaves were sometimes sold in Southeast Asia: see Furber, *Rival Empires of Trade*, p. 318 and his note 59; also, Pamela Gutman, "Arakan," in *Encyclopedia of Asian History* (New York: Charles Scribner's Sons, 1988).

58. Boxer, *The Portuguese Seaborne Empire*, pp. 138–140.

59. Edward A. Alpers, *Ivory and Slaves: Changing Pattern of International Trade in East Central Africa to the Later Nineteenth Century* (Berkeley: University of California Press, 1975), p. 95.

60. E.g., Risso, *Oman*, p. 82.

61. William Gervase Clarence-Smith, "The Economics of the Indian Ocean and Red Sea Slave Trades in the 19th Century: An Overview," in William Gervase Clarence-Smith, ed., *The Economics of the Indian Ocean Slave Trade in the Nineteenth Century* (London: Frank Cass, 1989), pp. 4 and 8.

62. Risso, *Oman*, pp. 126–129.

63. David Brion Davis, *Slavery and Human Progress* (New York: Oxford University Press, 1984), pp. 107–109.

64. Reid, "Introduction," in Reid, ed., *Slavery and Bondage*, pp. 4–5.

65. Davis, *Slavery and Human Progress*, pp. 136 and 108.

66. Most data available are from the nineteenth century. See, for example, Frederick Cooper, *Plantation Slavery on the East Coast of Africa* (New Haven: Yale University Press, 1977), pp. 38–46.

67. Allen, "Sayyids, Shets and Sultans," unpublished PhD dissertation, p. 157.

68. For a summary of Islamic regulation of slavery, see Lewis, *Race and Slavery in the Middle East*, ch. 1.

69. For an example of the use of these arguments in an essentially political dispute between the Ottoman central government and the provincial governor at Mecca, see Ehud R. Toledano, *The Ottoman Slave Trade and Its Suppression* (Princeton: Princeton University Press, 1982), pp. 129–135.

70. Landen, *Oman Since 1856*, ch. 4.

71. Tomé Pires, *The Suma Oriental: An Account of the East, from the Red Sea to Japan, written in Malacca and India in 1512–1515*, Armando Cortesão, trans. and ed. (London: The Hakluyt Society, 1944), vol. 1, p. 42.

72. Steensgaard, "The Indian Ocean Network," in Chandra, ed., *The Indian Ocean*, p. 135.

73. See note 14, this chapter.

74. M. N. Pearson, *Before Colonialism: Theories on Asian-European Relations 1500–1750* (Delhi: Oxford University Press, 1988), p. 25 and note 50. In this section, Pearson argues against Immanuel Wallerstein's inclusion of Asia in a single world system based on Western capitalism before the nineteenth century.

75. Sanjay Subrahmanyam formulates this historiographical contrast some-what differently, i.e., between forceful European dominance and friendly part-nership, and regards neither as adequate. He finds a middle ground in his char-acterization of European-Asian contact as "contained conflict." See *The Political Economy of Commerce*, ch. 5.

76. Piero Strozzi, quoted by Subrahmanyam, *The Political Economy of Commerce*, p. 7.

77. Furber, *Rival Empires of Trade*, p. 6.

78. Steensgaard, "The Indian Ocean Network," in Chandra, ed., *The Indian Ocean*, p. 128 including note 2.

Chapter 6

1. M. N. Pearson, "India and the Indian Ocean in the Sixteenth Century," in Ashin Das Gupta and M. N. Pearson, eds., *India and the Indian Ocean, 1500–1800* (Calcutta: Oxford University Press, 1987), p. 79. Also, see Chapter 4 in this volume, in text at note 14.

2. Sanjay Subrahmanyam, *The Political Economy of Commerce: Southern India, 1500–1650* (Cambridge: Cambridge University Press, 1990), e.g., p. 367.

3. Ibid., p. 298.

4. John F. Richards, review of Subrahmanyam's book, in *The American Historical Review*, vol. 96, no. 3 (June, 1991), p. 934. For an earlier era, S. D. Goitein, "The Rise of the Near-Eastern Bourgeoisie in Early Islamic Times," *Cahiers d'Histoire Mondiale*, vol. 3, part 3 (1957), p. 584.

5. See Chapter 2 in this volume, in text at note 34.

6. See, for example, Conrad Schirokauer, *A Brief History of Chinese and Japanese Civilizations*, 2nd edn. (San Diego: Harcourt Brace Jovanovich, Publishers, 1989), pp. 246 and 348–351.

7. For different views on peripheralization, see M. N. Pearson, *Before Colonialism: Theories on Asian-European Relations, 1500–1750* (Delhi: Oxford University Press, 1988) and Immanuel Wallerstein, "The Incorporation of the Indian Sub-continent into the Capitalist World-Economy," in Satish Chandra, ed., *The Indian Ocean: Explorations in History, Commerce and Politics* (New Delhi: Sage Publications, 1987).

8. For a discussion of various views on this issue, see Subrahmanyam, *The Political Economy of Commerce*, pp. 2–5. See also a Marxist historian of Islam, Maxime Rodinson, *Islam and Capitalism*, trans. by Brian Pearce (Austin: University of Texas Press, 1978), in which it is argued that Islam is compatible with, though not insistent upon, capitalism.

9. Subrahmanyam, *The Political Economy of Commerce*, pp. 5–6, including footnotes 10–13.

10. A classic on this controversial topic is Karl A. Wittfogel, *Oriental Despotism: A Comparative Study of Total Power* (New Haven: Yale University Press, 1957).

11. Subrahmanyam, *The Political Economy of Commerce*, pp. 6–7.

12. See Chapter 3 in this volume, note 15.

13. See Chapter 5 in this volume, in text at note 78.

14. Arun Das Gupta, "The Maritime Trade of Indonesia, 1500–1800," in Ashin Das Gupta and M. N. Pearson, eds., *India and the Indian Ocean, 1500–1800* (Cal-

cutta: Oxford University Press, 1987), p. 256. He also argues that the failure of all Muslims in Southeast Asia to defend Melaka against the Portuguese proves that there was no Muslim solidarity, ibid., p. 250. Yet, in his own description of events, it is evident that there were Muslims, including Ottoman mercenaries, on one side (with perhaps a few Hindu Gujarati allies) and non-Muslims on the other side: Portuguese, Chinese, Hindus. It is true that Javanese Muslims, who had been hurt by the rise of Melaka and who had attacked that port themselves before the Portuguese arrived, had little incentive to help defend the port. This is evidence against the existence of a *single* Muslim network but not against multiple Muslim networks or their hierarchic nature.

15. See Chapter 3 in this volume, in text at note 62.

16. See Chapter 4 in this volume, in text at notes 46 and 47.

17. See Chapter 5 in this volume, in text at note 40 and just after note 43.

18. E.g., Moojan Momen, *An Introduction to Shi'i Islam: The History and Doctrines of Twelver Shi'ism* (Oxford: George Ronald, 1985), p. 90.

19. For examples from the eighteenth century, see P. Risso, "Muslim Identity in Maritime Trade: General Observations and Some Evidence from the 18th-Century Persian Gulf/Indian Ocean Region," *International Journal of Middle East Studies,* vol. 21 (Aug., 1989), p. 385.

20. Chapter 5 in this volume, in text before note 47.

Bibliography

Abu-Lughod, Janet. *Before European Hegemony: The World System A.D. 1250–1350.* New York: Oxford University Press, 1989.

Aghassian, Michel and Kéram Kévonian. "Le commerce arménien dans l'Océan Indien aux 17e et 18e siècles," Denys Lombard and Jean Aubin, eds., *Marchands et hommes d'affaires asiatiques dans l'Océan Indien et la Mer de Chine 13e–20e siècles.* Paris: École des Hautes Études en Sciences Sociales, 1988.

Ahmad, S. Maqbul. "Ibn Madjid," *The Encyclopedia of Islam,* 2nd edn. Leiden: E. J. Brill, 1960–.

Algar, Hamid. "Kazruni," *The Encyclopedia of Islam,* 2nd edn. Leiden: E. J. Brill, 1960–.

Ali, Muhammad. *A Manual of Hadith.* Brooklyn, NY: Olive Branch Press, 1988.

Allen, Calvin. "The Indian Merchant Community of Masqat," *Bulletin of the School of Oriental and African Studies,* v. 44 (1981).

———. "Sayyids, Shets, and Sultans: Politics of Trade in Masqat Under the Al bu Sa'id, 1785–1914." Unpublished PhD dissertation, University of Washington (Seattle), 1978.

———. "The State of Masqat in the Gulf and East Africa, 1785–1829," *International Journal of Middle East Studies,* vol. 14, no. 2 (May, 1982).

Alpers, Edward A. *Ivory and Slaves: Changing Pattern of International Trade in East Central Africa to the Later Nineteenth Century.* Berkeley: University of California Press, 1975.

Andaya, Barbara Watson. *Perak, the Abode of Grace.* Kuala Lumpur: Oxford University Press, 1979.

———, and Yoneo Ishii. "Religious Developments in Southeast Asia, c. 1500–1800," Nicholas Tarling, ed., *The Cambridge History of Southeast Asia,* vol. 1, *From Early Times to c. 1800.* Cambridge: Cambridge University Press, 1992.

Arasaratnam, S. "India and the Indian Ocean in the Seventeenth Century," Ashin Das Gupta and M. N. Pearson, eds., *India and the Indian Ocean, 1500–1800.* Calcutta: Oxford University Press, 1987.

Ashtor, E. *Levant Trade in the Later Middle Ages.* Princeton: Princeton University Press, 1983.

———. *A Social and Economic History of the Near East in the Middle Ages.* Chicago: University of Chicago Press, 1974.

Atwell, William S. "A Seventeenth-Century 'General Crisis' in East Asia?" *Modern Asian Studies,* vol. 24, no. 4 (1990).

Aubin, Jean. "Marchands de Mer Rouge et du Golfe Persique au tournant des 15e et 16e siècles," Denys Lombard and Jean Aubin, eds., *Marchands et hommes*

d'affaires asiatiques dans l'Océan Indien et la Mer de Chine 13e–20e siècles.
Paris: École des Hautes Études en Sciences Sociales, 1988.

Austen, Ralph. *African Economic History.* London: James Currey and Portsmouth NH: Heinemann, 1987.

———. "The 19th Century Islamic Slave Trade from East Africa (Swahili and Red Sea Coasts): A Tentative Census," William Gervase Clarence-Smith, ed., *The Economics of the Indian Ocean Slave Trade in the Nineteenth Century.* London: Frank Cass, 1989.

Ayalon, David. "Bahriyya," section II, *The Encyclopedia of Islam.* 2nd edn. Leiden: E. J. Brill, 1960–.

———. *The Mamluk Military Society.* London, 1979.

Barbosa, Duarte. *The Book of Duarte Barbosa: An Account of the Countries Bordering on the Indian Ocean and Their Inhabitants, Written by Duarte Barbosa, and Completed About the Year 1518 A.D.,* trans. and ed. by Mansel Longworth Dames. 2 vols. London: The Hakluyt Society, 1918–1921.

Bathurst, R. D. "The Ya'rubi Dynasty of Oman." Unpublished DPhil dissertation, Oxford University, 1967.

Bayly, C. A. "India and West Asia, c. 1700–1830," *Asian Affairs,* vol. 19, no. 1 (Feb., 1988).

Beachey, R. W. *The Slave Trade of Eastern Africa.* London: Rex Collings, 1976.

Ben Shemesh, A. *Taxation in Islam,* 3 vols. Leiden: E. J. Brill and London: Luzac and Co. Ltd., 1958–1969.

Bentley, Jerry H. *Old World Encounters: Cross-Cultural Contacts and Exchanges in Pre-Modern Times.* New York: Oxford University Press, 1993.

Bhacker, M. Reda. *Trade and Empire in Muscat and Zanzibar: Roots of British Domination.* London and New York: Routledge, 1992.

Bhattacharya, S. "The Indian Ocean in the Nineteenth and Early Twentieth Centuries," Satish Chandra, ed., *The Indian Ocean: Explorations in History, Commerce and Politics.* New Delhi: Sage Publications, 1987.

Blussé, L., and R. Gaastra, eds. *Companies and Trade: Essays on Overseas Trading Companies During the Ancien Régime.* Leiden: Leiden University Press, 1981.

[Bonaparte, Napoléon.] *Correspondance inédite officielle et confidentielle de Napoléon Bonaparte avec les cours étrangères.* Paris, 1809–1820.

Bosworth, C. E. *The Ghaznavids.* Edinburgh: Edinburgh University Press, 1963.

Boxer, C. R. *Portuguese Conquest and Commerce in Southern Asia, 1500–1750.* London: Variorum Reprints, 1985. Collection of articles.

———. *The Portuguese Seaborn Empire, 1415–1825.* New York: Alfred A. Knopf, 1969.

Bouchon, Geneviève. *L'Asie du Sud à l'époque des Grandes Découvertes.* London: Variorum Reprints, 1987. Collection of her articles and papers.

———. "Un microcosme: Calicut au 16e siècle," Denys Lombard and Jean Aubin, eds., *Marchands et hommes d'affaires asiatiques dans l'Océan Indien et la Mer de Chine 13e–20e siècles.* Paris: École des Hautes Études en Sciences Sociales, 1988.

———. "Les Musulmans du Kerala à l'époque de la découverte portugaise," *L'Asie du Sud à l'époque des Grandes Découvertes.* London: Variorum Reprints, 1987.

_____. "Pour une histoire du Gujarat du XVe au XVIIe siècle," *L'Asie du Sud à l'époque des Grandes Découvertes.* London: Variorum Reprints, 1987.

_____. "Quelques aspects de l'Islamisation des régions maritimes de l'Inde à l'époque médiévale (XIIe–XVIe siècles)," Marc Gaborieu, ed., *Islam et Société en Asie du Sud.* Paris: École des Hautes Études en Sciences Sociales, 1986. (This also appears in *L'Asie du Sud à l'époque des Grandes Découvertes.* London: Variorum Reprints, 1987.)

_____. "Sixteenth Century Malabar and the Indian Ocean," in Ashin Das Gupta and M. N. Pearson, eds., *India and the Indian Ocean, 1500–1800.* Calcutta: Oxford University Press, 1987.

Braudel, Fernand. *Civilization and Capitalism, 15th–18th Century,* 3 vols., trans. by Sian Reynolds. New York: Harper and Row, 1982–1984.

_____. *The Mediterranean and the Mediterranean World in the Age of Philip II,* trans. by Sian Reynolds, 2 vols. New York: Harper and Row, 1972–1973.

Broeze, Frank, ed. *Brides of the Sea: Port Cities of Asia from the 16th–20th Centuries.* Honolulu: University of Hawaii Press, 1989.

Brunschvig, R. "'Abd," *The Encyclopedia of Islam,* 2nd edn., Leiden: E. J. Brill, 1960–.

Cahen, Claude. "Le commerce musulman dans l'Océan Indien au Moyen Age," Michel Mollat, ed., *Sociétés et compagnies de commerce en Orient et dans l'Océan Indien.* Paris: SEVPEN, 1970.

_____, et al. "Hisba," *The Encyclopedia of Islam,* 2nd edn. Leiden: E. J. Brill, 1960–.

_____. "Ikta'," *The Encyclopedia of Islam,* 2nd edn. Leiden: E. J. Brill, 1960–.

Calmard, Jean. "Les marchands iraniens," Denys Lombard and Jean Aubin, eds., *Marchands et hommes d'affaires asiatiques dans l'Océan Indien et la Mer de Chine 13e–20e siècles.* Paris: École des Hautes Études en Sciences Sociales, 1988.

Canard, M. "Fatimids," *The Encyclopedia of Islam,* 2nd edn. Leiden: E. J. Brill, 1960–.

Carswell, John. "The Armenians and East-West Trade Through Persia in the XVIIth Century," Michel Mollat, ed., *Sociétés et compagnies de commerce en Orient et dans l'Océan Indien.* Paris: SEVPEN, 1970.

Chandra, Satish, ed. *The Indian Ocean: Explorations in History, Commerce and Politics.* New Delhi: Sage Publications, 1987.

Chaudhuri, K. N. *Asia Before Europe: Economy and Civilisation of the Indian Ocean from the Rise of Islam to 1750.* Cambridge: Cambridge University Press, 1990.

_____. "Reflections on the Organizing Principle of Premodern Trade," James D. Tracy, ed., *The Political Economy of Merchant Empires.* Cambridge: Cambridge University Press, 1991.

_____. *Trade and Civilisation in the Indian Ocean: An Economic History from the Rise of Islam to 1750.* Cambridge: Cambridge University Press, 1985.

_____. *The Trading World of Asia and the English East India Company, 1660–1760.* Cambridge: Cambridge University Press, 1978.

Chittick, H. Neville, and Robert I. Rothberg, eds. *East Africa and the Orient: Cultural Syntheses in Pre-Colonial Times.* New York: Africana Publishing Co., 1975.

Clarence-Smith, William Gervase. "The Economics of the Indian Ocean and Red Sea Slave Trades in the 19th Century: An Overview," William Gervase Clarence-Smith, ed., *The Economics of the Indian Ocean Slave Trade in the Nineteenth Century.* London: Frank Cass, 1989.

———, ed. *The Economics of the Indian Ocean Slave Trade in the Nineteenth Century.* London: Frank Cass, 1989.

Coedès, G. *The Indianized States of Southeast Asia,* ed. by Walter F. Vella and trans. by Susan Brown Cowing. Honolulu: East-West Center Press, 1968.

Cooper, Frederick. *Plantation Slavery on the East Coast of Africa.* New Haven: Yale University Press, 1977.

Crone, Patricia. *Meccan Trade and the Rise of Islam.* Princeton: Princeton University Press, 1987.

———. *Slaves on Horses: The Evolution of the Islamic Polity.* Cambridge: Cambridge University Press, 1980.

Crossette, Barbara. "Sultan Died a Hero, but His Name Is Now Sullied in a Religious Dispute," *The New York Times.* Feb. 1, 1990, p. A4.

Curtin, Philip D. *Cross-Cultural Trade in World History.* Cambridge: Cambridge University Press, 1984.

Dale, Stephen Frederic. *Islamic Society on the South Asian Frontier: The Mappilas of Malabar, 1498–1922.* Oxford: Clarendon Press, 1980.

———. "Mappilas," *Encyclopedia of Asian History.* New York: Charles Scribner's Sons, 1988.

Das Gupta, Arun. "The Maritime Trade of Indonesia, 1500–1800," Ashin Das Gupta and M. N. Pearson, eds., *India and the Indian Ocean, 1500–1800.* Calcutta: Oxford University Press, 1987.

Das Gupta, Ashin, "Indian Merchants and the Trade of the Indian Ocean," Tapan Raychaudhuri and Irfan Habib, eds., *The Cambridge Economic History of India,* 2 vols., vol. 1, c. 1200–1750. Cambridge: Cambridge University Press, 1982.

———. "A Note on the Shipowning Merchants of Surat c. 1700," Denys Lombard and Jean Aubin, eds., *Marchands et hommes d'affaires asiatiques dans l'Océan Indien et la Mer de Chine 13e–20e siècles.* Paris: École des Hautes Études en Sciences Sociales, 1988.

———, and M. N. Pearson, eds. *India and the Indian Ocean, 1500–1800.* Calcutta: Oxford University Press, 1987.

Davis, David Brion. *Slavery and Human Progress.* New York: Oxford University Press, 1984.

Denny, Frederick Mathewson. *An Introduction to Islam,* 2nd edn. New York: Macmillan Publishing Company, 1994.

Dermigny, Louis. *La Chine et l'Occident: Le Commerce à Canton au XVIIIe siècle, 1719–1833,* 3 vols. Paris: SEVPEN, 1964.

Derry, T. K., and Trevor I. Williams. *A Short History of Technology from the Earliest Times to A.D. 1900.* Oxford: Clarendon Press, 1960.

Digby, Simon. "The Maritime Trade of India," Tapan Raychaudhuri and Irfan Habib, eds., *The Cambridge Economic History of India,* 2 vols., vol. 1, c. 1200–1750. Cambridge: Cambridge University Press, 1982.

Di Meglio, Rita R. "Arab Trade with Indonesia and the Malay Peninsula from the 8th to the 16th Century," D. S. Richards, ed., *Islam and the Trade of Asia*. Oxford: Bruno Cassirer, 1970.

Dols, Michael W. *The Black Death in the Middle East.* Princeton: Princeton University Press, 1977.

Donner, Fred McGraw. *The Early Islamic Conquests.* Princeton: Princeton University Press, 1981.

Dunn, Ross E. *The Adventures of Ibn Battuta: A Muslim Traveler of the 14th Century.* London: Croom Helm, 1986.

Ehrenkreutz, A. S. "Another Orientalist's Remarks Concerning the Pirenne Thesis," *Journal of the Economic and Social History of the Orient*, vol. 15 (1972).

_____. "Bahriyya," *The Encyclopedia of Islam*, 2nd edn., Supplement. Leiden: E. J. Brill, 1980.

Ellen, Roy F. "Social Theory, Ethnography and the Understanding of Practical Islam in South-East Asia," M. B. Hooker, ed., *Islam in Southeast Asia*. Leiden: E. J. Brill, 1983.

Endicott-West, Elizabeth. Review of Janet Abu-Lughod, *Before European Hegemony*, in *The Journal of Asian Studies*, vol. 49, no. 2 (May, 1990).

Fairbank, John K., ed., *The Chinese World Order: Traditional China's Foreign Relations.* Cambridge, MA: Harvard University Press, 1968.

_____, and Edwin O. Reischauer. *China: Tradition and Transformation*, revised edn. Boston: Houghton Mifflin Co., 1989.

Ferrand, G. *Relations de voyages et textes géographiques arabes, persans, et turks, relatif à l'Extrême-Orient du VIII au XVIII siècles*, 2 vols. Paris, 1913–1914.

Fletcher, Joseph F. "China and Central Asia, 1368–1884," John K. Fairbank, ed., *The Chinese World Order: Traditional China's Foreign Relations.* Cambridge, MA: Harvard University Press, 1968.

Furber, Holden. *Rival Empires of Trade in the Orient, 1600–1800.* Minneapolis: University of Minnesota Press, 1976.

Fyzee, A. A. A. "Bohoras," *The Encyclopedia of Islam*, 2nd edn. Leiden: E. J. Brill, 1960–.

Glamann, K. *Dutch-Asiatic Trade, 1620–1740.* Copenhagen, 1958.

Goitein, S. D. *A Mediterranean Society*, 3 vols., vol. 1, *Economic Foundations.* Berkeley: University of California Press, 1967.

_____. "The Rise of the Near-Eastern Bourgeoisie in Early Islamic Times," *Cahiers d'Histoire Mondiale*, vol. 3, part 3 (1957).

_____. *Studies in Islamic History and Institutions.* Leiden: E. J. Brill, 1966.

Golden, Peter B. "The Karakhanids and Early Islam," Denis Sinor, ed., *The Cambridge History of Early Inner Asia.* Cambridge: Cambridge University Press, 1990.

Goldstone, Jack A. "East and West in the Seventeenth Century: Political Crises in Stuart England, Ottoman Turkey, and Ming China," *Comparative Studies in Society and History*, vol. 30, no. 1 (Jan., 1988).

_____. *Revolution and Rebellion in the Early Modern World.* Berkeley: University of California Press, 1991.

Habib, Irfan. "Merchant Communities in Precolonial India," James D. Tracy, ed., *The Rise of Merchant Empires: Long-Distance Trade in the Early Modern World, 1350–1750.* Cambridge: Cambridge University Press, 1990.

Hall, Kenneth. *Maritime Trade and State Development in Early Southeast Asia.* Honolulu: University of Hawaii Press, 1985.

Hamilton, Alexander. *A New Account of the East Indies,* ed. by William Foster, 2 vols. London: The Argonaut Press, 1930 (originally published in 1727).

Hamonic, Gilbert. "Les réseaux marchands bugis-makassar," Denys Lombard and Jean Aubin, eds., *Marchands et hommes d'affaires asiatiques dans l'Océan Indien et la Mer de Chine 13e–20e siècles.* Paris: École des Hautes Études en Sciences Sociales, 1988.

Hasan, Mohibbul. *History of Tipu Sultan.* Calcutta: The World Press Private Ltd., 1971.

Havinghurst, Alfred E., ed., *The Pirenne Thesis: Analysis, Criticism, and Revision.* Boston: D. C. Heath and Company, 1958.

Heffening, W. "Sarf," *First Encyclopedia of Islam, 1913–1936.* Leiden: E. J. Brill, 1987.

Hess, Andrew. "The Evolution of the Ottoman Seaborne Empire in the Age of Oceanic Discoveries, 1453–1525," *The American Historical Review,* vol. 75 (Dec., 1970).

———. *The Forgotten Frontier: A History of the Sixteenth-Century Ibero-African Frontier.* Chicago: University of Chicago Press, 1978.

Hodgson, Marshall G. S. *The Venture of Islam.* 3 vols. Chicago: University of Chicago Press, 1974.

Hooker, M. B., ed. *Islam in South-East Asia.* Leiden: E. J. Brill, 1983.

Hourani, George. *Arab Seafaring in the Indian Ocean in Ancient and Medieval Times.* Princeton: Princeton University Press, 1951.

Hudson, G. F. "The Medieval Trade of China," D. S. Richards, eds., *Islam and the Trade of Asia.* Oxford: Bruno Cassirer, 1970.

Ibn Battuta, *Travels of Ibn Battuta A.D. 1325–1354,* 3 vols. Arabic text ed. by C. Defrémery and B. R. Sanguinetti, trans. by H. A. R. Gibb. Cambridge: The Hakluyt Society, 1962.

Ibn Khaldun, *The Muqaddimah: An Introduction to History,* trans. by Franz Rosenthal, ed. and abridged by N. J. Dawood. Princeton: Princeton University Press, 1969.

Ibrahim, Mahmood. *Merchant Capital and Islam.* Austin: University of Texas Press, 1990.

India Office Records, London: Bombay Political and Secret Proceedings and Bombay State Papers.

Islamoğlu-İnan, Hurî, ed. *The Ottoman Empire and the World-Economy.* Cambridge: Cambridge University Press, 1987.

Israeli, R. "Islamization and Sinicization in Chinese Islam," Nehemia Levtzion, ed., *Conversion to Islam.* New York: Holmes & Meier Publishers, Inc., 1979.

Itzkowitz, Norman, *Ottoman Empire and Islamic Tradition.* Chicago: University of Chicago Press, Phoenix Edition, 1980.

Jafri, Husain M. *Origins and Early Development of Shi'a Islam.* London: Longman Group Ltd., 1979.

Khachikian, Lvon. "The Ledger of the Merchant Hovannes Joughayetsi," *Journal of the Asiatic Society*, vol. 8, no. 3. (1966).

Khalidi, Tarif. *Islamic Historiography: The Histories of Mas'udi*. Albany: State University of New York Press, 1975.

Kirkpatrick, William, ed. and trans. *Select Letters of Tippoo Sultan*. London, 1811.

Kling, Blair B., and M. N. Pearson, eds. *The Age of Partnership: Europeans in Asia Before Dominion*. Honolulu: University of Hawaii Press, 1979.

Kunt, I. Metin. *The Sultan's Servants: The Transformation of Ottoman Provincial Government, 1550–1650*. New York: Columbia University Press, 1983.

Labib, S. Y. "Karimi," *The Encyclopedia of Islam*. 2nd edn. Leiden: E. J. Brill, 1960–.

_____. "Les Marchands Karimis en Orient et sur l'Océan Indien," Michel Mollat, ed., *Sociétés et compagnies de commerce en Orient et dans l'Océan Indien*. Paris: SEVPEN, 1970.

Landen, R. G. *Oman Since 1856: Disruptive Modernization in a Traditional Arab Society*. Princeton: Princeton University Press, 1967.

Langlois, John D., Jr., ed. *China Under Mongol Rule*. Princeton: Princeton University Press, 1981.

Leur, J. van. *Indonesian Trade and Society: Essays in Asian Social and Economic History*. The Hague: W. van Hoeve, 1955.

Levtzion, Nehemia, ed. *Conversion to Islam*. New York: Holmes and Meier Publishers, Inc., 1979.

Lewis, Archibald. "Les Marchands dans l'Océan Indien," *Revue d'Histoire Économiques et sociales*, vol. 54, no. 4 (1976).

_____. "Maritime Skills in the Indian Ocean, 1368–1500," *Journal of the Economic and Social History of the Orient*, vol. 16, parts 2 and 3 (1973).

_____. *Nomads and Crusaders, A.D. 1000–1368*. Bloomington: Indiana University Press, 1988.

Lewis, Bernard. "The Fatimids and the Route to India," *Revue de la Faculté des Sciences Économiques de l'Université d'Istanbul*, vol. 14 (1953).

_____. *The Muslim Discovery of Europe*. New York: W. W. Norton & Co., 1982.

_____. *Race and Slavery in the Middle East: An Historical Inquiry*. Oxford: Oxford University Press, 1992.

Lewis, Diane. "Melaka," *Encyclopedia of Asian History*. New York: Charles Scribner's Sons, 1988.

Lo, Jung-pang. "Chinese Shipping and East-West Trade from the Tenth to the Fourteenth Century," Michel Mollat, ed., *Sociétés et compagnies de commerce en Orient et dans l'Océan Indien*. Paris: SEVPEN, 1970.

_____. "Maritime Commerce and Its Relationship to the Sung Navy," *Journal of the Economic and Social History of the Orient*, vol. 12 (1969).

Lombard, Denys, and Jean Aubin, eds. *Marchands et hommes d'affaires asiatiques dans l'Océan Indien et la Mer de Chine 13e–20e siècles*. Paris: École des Hautes Études en Sciences Sociales, 1988.

Lombard, Maurice. *The Golden Age of Islam*, trans. by Joan Spencer. Amsterdam: North-Holland Publishing Company, 1975.

Ma Huan. *Ying-Yai Sheng-Lan, "The Overall Survey of the Ocean's Shores" (1433),* trans. and introduced by J. V. G. Mills. Cambridge: The Hakluyt Society, 1970.

MacLean, Derryl. *Religion and Society in Arab Sind.* Leiden: E. J. Brill, 1989.

Madelung, W. "Khodja," *The Encyclopedia of Islam,* 2nd edn. Leiden: E. J. Brill, 1960–.

Makdisi, George. "The Sunni Revival," D. S. Richards, ed., *Islamic Civilisation, 950–1150.* Oxford: Bruno Cassirer Ltd., 1973.

Manguin, Peirre-Yves. "The Vanishing *Jong:* Insular Southeast Asian Fleets in Trade and War (Fifteenth to Seventeenth Centuries)," Anthony Reid, ed., *Southeast Asia in the Early Modern Era: Trade, Power and Belief.* Ithaca, NY: Cornell University Press, 1993.

Masters, Bruce. *The Origins of Western Economic Dominance in the Middle East: Mercantilism and the Islamic Economy in Aleppo, 1600–1750.* New York: New York University Press, 1988.

McNeill, William H. *Plagues and Peoples.* Garden City, NY: Anchor Press/ Doubleday, 1976.

———. *The Pursuit of Power: Technology, Armed Force and Society Since A.D. 1000.* Oxford: Basil Blackwell, 1983.

Meilink-Roelofsz, M. A. P. *Asian Trade and European Influence in the Indonesian Archipelago Between 1500 and About 1630.* The Hague: Martinus Nijhoff, 1962.

———. "Trade and Islam in the Malay-Indonesian Archipelago Prior to the Arrival of the Europeans," D. S. Richards, ed., *Islam and the Trade of Asia.* Oxford: Bruno Cassirer, 1970.

Mollat, Michel, ed. *Sociétés et compagnies de commerce en Orient et dans l'Océan Indien.* Paris: SEVPEN, 1970.

Momen, Moojan. *An Introduction to Shi'i Islam: The History and Doctrines of Twelver Shi'ism.* Oxford: George Ronald, 1985.

Mookerji, Radhakumud. *Indian Shipping: A History of the Sea-Borne Trade and Maritime Activity of the Indian Ocean from the Earliest Times.* Bombay: Longmans, Green and Co., 1912.

Moreland, W. H. *From Akbar to Aurangzeb: A Study in Indian Economic History.* New Delhi: Oriental Reprint Corporation, 1972 (originally published in 1923).

Morgan, David. *Medieval Persia, 1040–1797.* London: Longman, 1988.

Morony, Michael G. *Iraq After the Muslim Conquest.* Princeton: Princeton University Press, 1984.

Nightingale, Pamela. *Trade and Empire in Western India, 1784–1806.* Cambridge: Cambridge University Press, 1970.

O'Brien, Patrick. "European Economic Development: The Contribution of the Periphery," *The Economic History Review,* vol. 35, no. 1 (Feb., 1982).

Olschki, Leonardo. *Marco Polo's Asia: An Introduction to His "Description of the World" called "Il Milione."* Berkeley: University of California Press, 1960.

Palat, Ravi, Kenneth Barr, James Matson, Vinay Bahl, and Nesar Ahmad. "The Incorporation and Peripheralization of South Asia, 1600–1950," *Review,* A Journal of the Fernand Braudel Center for the Study of Economics, Historical Systems, and Civilizations, vol. 10, no. 1 (Summer, 1986).

Panikkar, K. M. *Asia and Western Dominance: A Survey of the Vasco Da Gama Epoch of Asian History, 1498–1945,* 2nd edn. London: George Allen & Unwin Ltd, 1959.

Parry, J. H. *The Establishment of the European Hegemony, 1415–1715: Trade and Exploration in the Age of the Renaissance,* 3rd edn. New York: Harper & Row Publishers, Harper Torchbooks, 1966.

Parsons, Abraham. *Travels in Asia and Africa.* London, 1808.

Pearson, M. N. *Before Colonialism: Theories on Asian-European Relations 1500–1750.* Delhi: Oxford University Press, 1988.

_____. "Calicut," *Encyclopedia of Asian History.* New York: Charles Scribner's Sons, 1988.

_____. "India and the Indian Ocean in the Sixteenth Century," Ashin Das Gupta and M. N. Pearson, eds., *India and the Indian Ocean, 1500–1800.* Calcutta: Oxford University Press, 1987.

_____. *Merchants and Rulers in Gujarat: The Response to the Portuguese in the Sixteenth Century.* Berkeley: University of California Press, 1976.

_____. "Merchants and States," James D. Tracy, ed., *The Political Economy of Merchant Empires.* Cambridge: Cambridge University Press, 1991.

Piekaar, A. J. "Atjeh," second section of entry. *The Encyclopedia of Islam,* 2nd edn. Leiden: E. J. Brill, 1960–.

Pipes, Daniel. *Slave Soldiers and Islam.* New Haven: Yale University Press, 1981.

Pirenne, Henri. *Mohammed and Charlemagne,* trans. by B. Miall. New York: W. W. Norton, 1939.

Pires, Tomé. *The Suma Oriental: An Account of the East, from the Red Sea to Japan, Written in Malacca and India in 1512–1515,* 2 vols., trans. and ed. by Armando Cortesão. London: The Hakluyt Society, 1944.

Prakash, Om. "The Dutch East India Company in the Trade of the Indian Ocean," Ashin Das Gupta and M. N. Pearson, eds., *India and the Indian Ocean, 1500–1800.* Calcutta: Oxford University Press, 1987.

Rahman, Fazlur. *Islam,* 2nd edn. Chicago: University of Chicago Press, 1979.

Ray, Harapsad. "China and the 'Western Ocean' in the Fifteenth Century," Satish Chandra, ed., *The Indian Ocean: Explorations in History, Commerce and Politics.* New Delhi: Sage Publications, 1987.

Raychaudhuri, Tapan, and Irfan Habib. *The Cambridge History of India,* 2 vols, vol. 1, c. 1200–1750. Cambridge: Cambridge University Press, 1982.

Raymond, André. *Artisans et commerçants au Caire au XVIIIe siècle.* Damascus: Institut français de Damas, 1973–1974.

Reid, Anthony. "Introduction: Slavery and Bondage in Southeast Asian History," Anthony Reid, ed., *Slavery, Bondage and Dependency in Southeast Asia.* New York: St. Martin's Press, 1983.

_____. "Islamization and Christianization in Southeast Asia: The Critical Phase, 1550–1650," Anthony Reid, ed., *Southeast Asia in the Early Modern Era: Trade, Power and Belief.* Ithaca, NY: Cornell University Press, 1993.

_____. *Southeast Asia in the Age of Commerce, 1450–1680,* 2 vols. vol. 1, *The Lands Below the Winds.* New Haven: Yale University Press, 1988; vol. 2, *Expansion and Crisis.* New Haven: Yale University Press, 1993.

_____, ed. *Southeast Asia in the Early Modern Era: Trade, Power and Belief.* Ithaca, NY: Cornell University Press, 1993.

_____, ed. *Slavery, Bondage and Dependency in Southeast Asia.* New York: St. Martin's Press, 1983.

Richards, D. S., ed. *Islam and the Trade of Asia.* Oxford: Bruno Cassirer, 1970.

_____, ed. *Islamic Civilisation, 950–1150.* Oxford: Bruno Cassirer Ltd., 1973.

Richards, John F. *The New Cambridge History of India,* part 1, vol. 5, *The Mughal Empire.* Cambridge: Cambridge University Press, 1993.

_____. Review of Sanjay Subrahmanyam, *The Political Economy of Commerce,* in *The American Historical Review,* vol. 96, no. 3 (June, 1991).

Ricks, Thomas Miller. "Politics and Trade in Southern Iran and the Gulf, 1745–1765." Unpublished PhD dissertation, Indiana University, 1974.

Risso, P. "Muslim Identity in Maritime Trade: General Observations and Some Evidence from the 18th-Century Persian Gulf/Indian Ocean Region," *International Journal of Middle East Studies,* vol. 21 (1989).

_____. *Oman and Muscat: An Early Modern History.* London: Croom Helm and New York: St. Martin's Press, 1986.

_____ [Dubuisson]. "Qasimi Piracy and the General Treaty of Peace (1820)," *Arabian Studies,* vol. 4 (1978).

Rodinson, Maxime. *Islam and Capitalism,* trans. by Brian Pearce. Austin: University of Texas Press, 1978.

Rossabi, Morris, ed. *China Among Equals: The Middle Kingdom and Its Neighbors, 10th–14th Centuries.* Berkeley: University of California Press, 1983.

_____. "The 'Decline' of the Central Asian Caravan Trade," James D. Tracy, ed., *The Rise of Merchant Empires: Long-Distance Trade in the Early Modern World, 1350–1750.* Cambridge: Cambridge University Press, 1990.

_____. "Muslim and Central Asian Revolts," Jonathan D. Spence and John E. Wills, Jr., eds., *From Ming to Ch'ing: Conquest, Region and Continuity in Seventeenth-Century China.* New Haven: Yale University Press, 1979.

_____. "The Muslims in the Early Yuan Dynasty," John D. Langlois, ed., *China Under Mongol Rule.* Princeton: Princeton University Press, 1981.

Rothermund, Dietmar. *Asian Trade and European Expansion in the Age of Mercantilism.* New Delhi: Manohar, 1981.

Sachedina, Abdulaziz Abdulhussein. *The Just Ruler (al-sultan al-'adil) in Shi'ite Islam.* New York: Oxford University Press, 1988.

SarDesai, D. R. *Southeast Asia, Past and Present.* 2nd edn. Boulder, CO: Westview Press, 1989.

Sauvaget, J., ed. and trans. *Ahbar as-Sin wa l-Hind: Relation de la Chine et de l'Inde.* Paris, 1948.

Savory, Roger. *Iran Under the Safavids.* Cambridge: Cambridge University Press, 1980.

Schafer, Edward H. *The Golden Peaches of Samarkand: A Study of T'ang Exotics.* Berkeley: University of California Press, 1963.

Schirokauer, Conrad. *A Brief History of Chinese and Japanese Civilizations,* 2nd edn. San Diego: Harcourt Brace Jovanovich, Publishers, 1989.

Serjeant, R. B. "Maritime Customary Law Off the Arabian Coasts," Michel Mollat, ed., *Sociétés et companies de commerce en Orient et dans l'Océan Indien.* Paris: SEVPEN, 1970.

_____. "Yemeni Merchants and Trade in Yemen, 13th–16th Centuries," Denys Lombard and Jean Aubin, eds., *Marchands et hommes d'affaires asiatiques dans l'Océan Indien et la Mer de Chine 13e–20e siècles.* Paris: École des Hautes Études en Sciences Sociales, 1988.

Shaban, M. A. *Islamic History: A New Interpretation,* vol. 1, A.D. 600–750 (A.H. 132). Cambridge: Cambridge University Press, 1971.

Shaw, Stanford J. *History of the Ottoman Empire and Modern Turkey,* 2 vols., vol. 1, *Empire of the Gazis: The Rise and Decline of the Ottoman Empire, 1280–1808.* Cambridge: Cambridge University Press, 1976.

Sheriff, A. "Localisation and Social Composition of the East African Slave Trade, 1858–1873," William Gervase Clarence-Smith, ed., *The Economics of the Indian Ocean Slave Trade in the Nineteenth Century.* London: Frank Cass, 1989.

Simkin, C. G. F. *The Traditional Trade of Asia.* London: Oxford University Press, 1968.

Sinor, Denis, ed. *The Cambridge History of Early Inner Asia.* Cambridge: Cambridge University Press, 1990.

Souza, G. B. "Maritime Trade and Politics in China and the South China Sea," Ashin Das Gupta and M. N. Pearson, eds., *India and the Indian Ocean, 1500–1800.* Calcutta: Oxford University Press, 1987.

Spence, Jonathan D., and John E. Wills, Jr., eds., *From Ming to Ch'ing: Conquest, Region and Continuity in Seventeenth-Century China.* New Haven: Yale University Press, 1979.

Steensgaard, Niels. *The Asian Trade Revolution of the Seventeenth Century: The East India Companies and the Decline of the Caravan Trade.* Chicago: University of Chicago Press, 1974.

_____. "The Indian Ocean Network and the Emerging World-Economy, c. 1500–1750," Satish Chandra, ed., *The Indian Ocean: Explorations in History, Commerce and Politics.* New Delhi: Sage Publications, 1987.

Stein, Burton. *The New Cambridge History of India,* part 1, vol. 3, *Vijayanagar.* Cambridge: Cambridge University Press, 1990.

_____. "South India: Some General Considerations of the Region and Its Early History," Tapan Raychaudhuri and Irfan Habib, eds., *The Cambridge Economic History of India,* vol. 1, c. 1200–c. 1750. Cambridge: Cambridge University Press, 1982.

_____. "Vijayanagar c. 1350–1564," Tapan Raychaudhur: and Irfan Habib, eds., *The Cambridge Economic History of India,* vol. 1, c. 1200–c. 1750. Cambridge: Cambridge University Press, 1982.

Stevens, Robert. *The New and Complete Guide to the East India Trade.* London, 1775.

Strenziok, G. "Azd," *The Encyclopedia of Islam,* 2nd edn., Leiden: E. J. Brill, 1960–.

Subrahmanyam, Sanjay. *The Political Economy of Commerce: Southern India, 1500–1650.* Cambridge: Cambridge University Press, 1990.

_____ and Luis Filipe Thomaz, "Evolution of Empire: The Portuguese in the Indian Ocean During the Sixteenth Century," James D. Tracy, ed. *The Political Economy of Merchant Empires*. Cambridge: Cambridge University Press, 1991.

Sutton, John E. G. *A Thousand Years of East Africa*. Nairobi: British Institute in Eastern Africa, 1990.

Tarling, Nicholas, ed. *The Cambridge History of Southeast Asia*, vol. 1, *From Early Times to c. 1800*. Cambridge: Cambridge University Press, 1992.

Thomaz, Luis Filipe. "Malaka et ses communautés marchandes au tournant du 16e siècle," Denys Lombard and Jean Aubin, eds., *Marchands et hommes d'affaires asiatiques dans l'Océan Indien et la Mer de Chine 13e–20e siècles*. Paris: École des Hautes Études en Sciences Sociales, 1988.

_____. "The Malay Sultanate of Melaka," Anthony Reid, ed., *Southeast Asia in the Early Modern Era: Trade, Power and Belief*. Ithaca, NY: Cornell University Press, 1993.

Tibbetts, G. R. *A Study of the Arabic Texts Containing Material on South-East Asia*. Leiden: E. J. Brill, 1979.

Toledano, Ehud R. *The Ottoman Slave Trade and Its Suppression: 1840–1890*. Princeton: Princeton University Press, 1982.

Toussaint, Auguste. *History of the Indian Ocean*, trans. by June Guicharnaud. Chicago: University of Chicago Press, 1966.

Tracy, James D., ed. *The Political Economy of Merchant Empires*. Cambridge: Cambridge University Press, 1991.

_____, ed. *The Rise of Merchant Empires: Long-Distance Trade in the Early Modern World, 1350–1750*. Cambridge: Cambridge University Press, 1990.

Trimingham, J. Spencer. *Islam in East Africa*. Oxford: Clarendon Press, 1964.

_____. *The Sufi Orders of Islam*. London: Oxford University Press, 1973.

Udovitch, Abraham. *Partnership and Profit in Medieval Islam*. Princeton: Princeton University Press, 1970.

Wake, C. "Malacca's Early Kings and the Reception of Islam," *Journal of Southeast Asian History*, vol. 2 (1964).

Walker, Paul E. "Bohoras," *Encyclopedia of Asian History*. New York: Charles Scribner's Sons, 1988.

_____. "Khojas," *Encyclopedia of Asian History*. New York: Charles Scribner's Sons, 1988.

Wallerstein, Immanuel. "The Incorporation of the Indian Subcontinent into the Capitalist World-Economy," Satish Chandra, ed., *The Indian Ocean: Explorations in History, Commerce and Politics*. New Delhi: Sage Publications, 1987.

_____. *The Modern World System*. New York: Academic Press, 1974–.

_____. Review of Janet Abu-Lughod, *Before European Hegemony*, in *International Journal of Middle East Studies*, vol. 24, no. 1 (Feb., 1992).

Wang Gungwu. "Merchants without Empire: The Hokkien Sojourning Communities," James D. Tracy, ed., *The Rise of Merchant Empires: Long-Distance Trade in the Early Modern World, 1350–1750*. Cambridge: Cambridge University Press, 1990.

Watt, William Montgomery. *Muhammad at Mecca*. Oxford: Clarendon Press, 1983.

Williams, Lea E. *Southeast Asia: A History.* New York: Oxford University Press, 1976.

Wills, John E., Jr. "Maritime China from Wang Chih to Shih Lang: Themes in Peripheral History," Jonathan D. Spence and John E. Wills, Jr., eds., *From Ming to Ch'ing: Conquest, Region and Continuity in Seventeenth-Century China.* New Haven: Yale University Press, 1979.

Wink, André. *Al-Hind: The Making of the Indo-Islamic World,* vol. 1, *Early Medieval India and the Expansion of Islam, 7th–11th Centuries.* Leiden: E. J. Brill, 1990.

Wolpert, Stanley. *A New History of India,* 4th edn. New York: Oxford University Press, 1993.

Wolters, O. W. *Early Indonesian Commerce.* Ithaca, NY: Cornell University Press, 1967.

Yoshinobu, Shiba. "Song Foreign Trade: Its Scope and Organization," Morris Rossabi, ed., *China Among Equals: The Middle Kingdom and Its Neighbors, 10th–14th Centuries.* Berkeley: University of California Press, 1983.

Yule, Henry, and A. C. Burnell. *Hobson-Jobson: A Glossary of Colloquial Anglo-Indian Words and Phrases ...,* 2nd edn., ed. by William Crooke. Delhi: Munshiram Manoharlal, 1968.

About the Book and Author

The intersection of Islamic history and Indian Ocean history is vast but inadequately explored. It is essential to understanding how and why Islam influenced Asia and to determining the extent to which maritime success affected the mostly land-based Muslim political powers. This area of research has elicited a lively debate involving scholars as diverse as William McNeill, K. N. Chaudhuri, Niels Steensgaard, Philip Curtin, and Janet Abu-Lughod. *Merchants and Faith* provides an insightful overview of this debate and addresses the major questions raised by it: What were the relationships between littoral Asia and land-based empires? How can we best explain the role played by West Europeans? What difference did it make to be a *Muslim* merchant? Other considerations are the production roles of China and Hindu India and the nature of the Asian trade revolution.

General histories of Islamic Asia seldom draw upon the rich literature on the Indian Ocean region; Indian Ocean studies are often couched in the technical jargon of economic theories and are occasionally marred by ideological bias. To make all of this literature more accessible to a general audience and to students, *Merchants and Faith* distills the results and implications of this research and connects them to the well-established features of Islamic political history.

Patricia Risso is associate professor of history at the University of New Mexico.

Index

Merchants and Faith